Code and Coin

Code and Coin

The Future of Money Beyond Governments

Nicolette Sharma

Mindful Pages

Published in 2026

ISBN: 9789374596340(PB)
ISBN: 9789374598382 (eBook)

Published by

Mindful Pages
Imprint of Alpha Editions LLC
312 W. 2nd St #1834
Casper, WY 82601, USA

Code and Coin

The Future of Money Beyond Governments

Nicolette Sharma

Mindful Pages

Published in 2026

ISBN: 9789374596340(PB)
ISBN: 9789374598382 (eBook)

Published by

Mindful Pages
Imprint of Alpha Editions LLC
312 W. 2nd St #1834
Casper, WY 82601, USA

This book was developed using advanced writing tools to support the drafting and ideation process. All content has been thoughtfully curated, refined, and reviewed to ensure quality and relevance.

Content

Introduction
The Code and the Coin

In the summer of 1696, English officials armed with scissors and sovereign power began to clip the edges off silver coins. The gesture was both desperate and ingenious: a wartime government quietly shaving its money to fund the crown's debts. Every clipped shilling was a small betrayal wrapped in necessity. Three centuries later, our governments have traded metal for code, but the impulse endures. We still clip value—through inflation that seeps like fog, through capital controls disguised as prudence, through algorithms whose opacity rivals any royal mint's secrecy. Money has always been a story of authority finding new instruments to command trust, and of subjects finding new ways to escape it.

This book begins with that paradox: that money is both a promise and a weapon, both a social covenant and a technology of control. What we call "digital currency" is not a simple payment innovation; it is an argument about the constitution of value itself. The contest between code and coin is not merely technical—it is political, philosophical, and increasingly existential. For the first time in centuries, the right to issue, police, and surveil money is being renegotiated not by parliaments or central banks, but by networks of miners, validators, and developers scattered across the globe. Their code is, in a sense, a constitution without a state. And yet, like all constitutions, it encodes power: who can change the rules, who can enforce them, and who is left out of the ledger entirely.

The chapters that follow treat money as an evolving protocol of governance. Each era has rewritten its monetary code to defend its prevailing order—from monarchs stamping coins with their faces to republics stamping laws upon paper, and now, to blockchains stamping consensus into mathematics. The form changes; the power struggles remain. This is why we must examine programmable money not as a technical curiosity but as a civilisational pivot. It redefines who may create, censor, or surveil economic life, and under what constraints. What hangs in the balance is not simply efficiency or convenience, but the architecture of freedom itself.

We live, uncomfortably, in a hybrid age. A citizen in Lagos trades stablecoins pegged to the dollar to protect against inflation; a bureaucrat in Brussels drafts code for a Central Bank Digital Currency; a miner in Kazakhstan secures Bitcoin blocks against states he will never see. Each actor believes they are pursuing rational goals—profit, control, security—but together they are rewriting the operating system of global value. Whether we like it or not, the new monetary order will be programmable. The question is by whom, and to what end.

To engage that question, one must first see money for what it is: not an inert medium of exchange, but an institutional design competing under pressure. The pound, the dollar, the yuan, the Bitcoin protocol—all are attempts to encode trust, discipline behaviour, and allocate permission. They are social technologies as much as technical ones, each optimised for a different blend of power, promises, and permissions. This book offers a framework for evaluating them on their own terms: by their governance (who sets the rules), their incentives (why the system persists), and their attack surfaces (how it might fail). The reader will not find here investment advice, evangelism, or prophecy. What is offered instead is a lens: a way to think rigorously about what makes a monetary system durable—or dangerously brittle.

To understand the new, we must first make peace with the old. The state did not invent money by decree; it evolved it through necessity. Medieval tallies and Renaissance bills of exchange were software before software—ledgers binding subjects and rulers in a shared illusion of value. Seigniorage, taxation, and credit were the original APIs of power, translating sovereignty into spreadsheets centuries before Excel. When crises came, governments bent their own rules to preserve survival. Elasticity, not honesty, became the mark of a resilient monetary regime. Yet every such act—whether suspending gold convertibility or issuing fiat currency—deepened the tension between rule and discretion, between trust and control. Bitcoin's emergence, centuries later, was less a revolution than a counter-reformation: a protest against monetary discretion written in the language of cryptography.

Bitcoin, of course, promised credible rules without a ruler. It replaced institutional trust with probabilistic truth, governed by mathematics rather than ministries. But this design came at a price: energy costs, latency, and social ossification. It proved that decentralisation was possible—but also that neutrality is expensive. Ethereum, the next great experiment, asked a different question: what if money could compute? In expanding the ledger to a universal machine, it multiplied both creativity and fragility. Its smart contracts, decentralised organisations, and algorithmic assets turned financial systems into living organisms—dynamic yet prone to cascade failures. The lesson is sobering: programmability magnifies both human ingenuity and human error.

While decentralised protocols sought independence from the state, the state studied their code and began to write its own. Central Bank Digital Currencies, or CBDCs, represent the mirror image of Bitcoin's rebellion: programmable money under public command. Their advocates promise efficiency, inclusion, and transparency; their critics warn of surveillance and behavioural control. The truth, as usual, lies in the architecture. Code does not only execute—it legislates. A CBDC can be designed to empower or to police, to protect citizens or to pre-empt them. Every design choice—retail or wholesale, direct or intermediated—translates into a political stance about who should see, stop, or steer a transaction.

Meanwhile, stablecoins quietly anchor the digital economy to the old world's gravity: the dollar. Their rise has made clear that the frontier still answers to empire. Wrapped in code and audited by algorithms, they are still promissory notes backed by traditional assets, serving users in unstable economies while deepening the dollar's reach. Disruption, paradoxically, has become conservation. The periphery adopts these digital dollars first, not out of ideology but necessity. For them, crypto is not speculation; it is survival.

What unites all these experiments—Bitcoin's purity, Ethereum's complexity, CBDCs' control, and stablecoins' mimicry—is a deeper design question: how do we build money that resists capture? Every ledger faces the same adversaries: the censor, the insider, the exploiter, the monopolist. Freedom in monetary design is not a slogan; it is a function of architecture. True independence depends not on slogans about decentralisation but on credible exit, diverse custody, and user-level sovereignty. Governance is not a committee but a code path; privacy is not a default but a price; usability is not convenience but politics in disguise.

The age of code-based money confronts us, then, with a mirror. Our financial systems reflect our collective appetites—for control, for security, for simplicity, for trust. Programmable money merely renders those appetites executable. The tension between freedom and order, anonymity and accountability, elasticity and discipline, will not be resolved by software. But software can make those tensions visible, and thus negotiable. In that sense, the new monetary revolution is less about replacing banks than about forcing societies to decide what they truly value.

If history offers any guidance, it is this: monetary systems endure not because they are perfect, but because they are adaptive. Empires fell when their money stopped encoding credible promises. Republics rose when citizens demanded visibility into how value was defined. Today, the same negotiation begins again, but with different tools. Our ledgers are global, our code open-source, our trust fragmented across thousands of nodes. We are, collectively, designing the next chapter of monetary civilisation. Whether it reads as emancipation or enclosure depends on how well we understand the stakes.

This book is an invitation to think like a constitutional engineer rather than a trader or a technologist. It asks the reader to examine not which token will rise, but which design can last. It proposes that the most radical act in an age of programmable value is not to speculate, but to understand. Each chapter equips you with a way to evaluate digital currencies as institutions under stress—whether issued by a state, a corporation, or a community. You will learn to read incentives as blueprints, to recognise fragility in tranquillity, to see ideology where others see only interface. Above all, you will learn to discern the difference between freedom encoded and freedom proclaimed.

The code and the coin are converging. Between them lies the future of money—and, perhaps, the future of power itself. This is not a book about technology; it is a book about the design of trust. And in a world where code now writes the rules, understanding that design is not optional. It is civic literacy for the twenty-first century.

Chapter 1
The First Protocol: How States Invented Money

In the chill of medieval England's winters, farmers would bring their taxes not in coin but in wooden sticks. Each tally was split in two: one half kept by the Crown, the other by the taxpayer. The notches carved along the edge recorded debts owed and payments made. Neither piece alone proved anything; together they verified a shared truth. This primitive ledger, backed by royal authority, was the first synchronised protocol of value—a way for the state to encode obligation, enforce memory, and materialise trust. Long before bytes and blockchains, the English Exchequer had already grasped that money was not a substance but a system. The tally stick's durability lay not in its oak grain but in its social architecture: two halves, one record, one rule.

Every civilisation has devised its own version of the tally stick. Whether stamped in bronze, chiselled in stone, or inked in ledgers, money began as a mechanism of coordination under authority. It solved the problem of trust at scale. The monarch's coin did not circulate because it was shiny or scarce, but because it bore a sovereign signature that linked value to command. Taxation completed the loop: the state issued currency into circulation and then demanded its return through tax. The result was a closed circuit of value, obligation, and control. Every coin carried both a face and a threat—the ruler's image on one side, the implicit promise of enforcement on the other. Money was governance in metal form.

From this vantage, seigniorage—the profit made by minting currency above its material cost—was never an accidental privilege. It was the design feature that sustained the system. By controlling issuance, rulers extracted economic rent in exchange for maintaining order and liquidity. The very act of minting established hierarchy: to issue money was to sit above those who merely used it. Modern states still defend this prerogative with near-religious zeal. Inflation, interest rates, and monetary policy are simply updated instruments of seigniorial power. What began as silver debasement has become digital debasement, but the logic endures: those who write the rules of value control the game itself. Understanding that continuity is vital, because today's blockchains challenge not the instrument of money but the authority to define it.

Beneath every monetary system lies an institutional bargain. The state offers stability, protection, and recognisable units of account; citizens, in turn, accept the state's monopoly on creating legal tender. This arrangement, forged in the crucible of empire and bureaucracy, allowed societies to scale. Money became the first operating system for civilisation, running silently beneath trade, law, and war. Yet the code was always proprietary. Its maintainers—kings, treasurers, central bankers—guarded their permissions fiercely. When new competitors emerge, from Renaissance bankers to twenty-first century cryptographers, they are treated not as innovators but as insurgents. The contest over money's code has always been a contest over sovereignty.

The myth that money derives its value from metal has long obscured its deeper truth: money is credit, not commodity. It is the promise that others will accept your promise. Gold coins and banknotes merely cloak that social fiction in physical or institutional form. When Florentine merchants in the fifteenth century began clearing debts through book entries rather than bullion, they discovered that reputation could substitute for rarity. A banker's ledger became more powerful than any vault of gold. What mattered was not the metal's hardness but the network's credibility. When governments later tied currencies to gold, they were less restoring honesty than outsourcing trust—to geology, rather than human discipline. The gold standard's allure was aesthetic: the comfort of believing that value could be measured by mass. Yet even in that golden age, credit quietly governed the system. The gold was symbolic; the promise was real.

This distinction between settlement and belief matters profoundly. When a Renaissance banker finalised a transaction, the settlement was social, not physical—trust in the intermediary replaced the exchange of metal. Similarly, when a blockchain finalises a block, the settlement is probabilistic—secured by computation, not coercion. Both are trust mechanisms, differently engineered. Understanding that continuum prepares us to evaluate modern claims of "credibly neutral" settlement. Neutrality is never absolute; it is designed, maintained, and contested. The myth of neutrality—whether in gold or code—conceals the political architecture that makes it possible.

History's great monetary ruptures have never been purely technical; they are crises of legitimacy. When wars drain treasuries or pandemics paralyse economies, states break their own rules to survive. The gold standard's suspension in 1914, Roosevelt's confiscation of gold in 1933, Nixon's closing of the dollar's convertibility in 1971—each was framed as temporary necessity but became permanent precedent. Elasticity, once introduced, is addictive. Rules give confidence, but discretion buys endurance. Every crisis thus reveals money's dual nature: a tool of discipline and a valve of survival. The state's willingness to bend its own constraints is both its strength and its moral hazard. It endures precisely because it can cheat without collapsing. For citizens, this elasticity poses a timeless question: do we prefer brittle integrity or adaptive stability? That question echoes today in the rivalry between algorithmic currencies that cannot yield and central banks that must.

To make sense of these shifting forms, this book introduces a diagnostic schema: *Power, Promises, Permissions*. *Power* defines who can issue or alter money. *Promises* define the rules of its value—convertibility, supply, stability. *Permissions* define who may access and use it, under what conditions. Every monetary design can be mapped along these axes. Adjust one, and the others react. Widen permissions without adjusting power, and you invite chaos. Strengthen promises without flexibility, and you risk collapse. Every society negotiates its own equilibrium. Understanding this interplay allows us to evaluate not only how money functions but whom it serves. Power structures, moralities, and market designs are encoded in the same lines of institutional code.

Seen through this lens, the history of money is less about economic evolution than about constitutional design. The move from tally sticks to blockchain ledgers is not a technological leap but a governance shift. Each generation redefines the boundaries between issuer and user, rule and exception, surveillance and freedom. The ancient tally stick taught two enduring lessons: that trust can be split and recombined, and that the state's half of the ledger always weighs heavier. Blockchains, for all their novelty, simply invite us to reimagine that balance without the monarch's seal. They are institutional competitors, not mere instruments—proposals for how societies might coordinate without kings.

As we step into this chapter, consider the enduring tension at its core: the state's need for elasticity versus the individual's need for certainty. Across centuries, that tension has driven innovation and abuse alike. The systems that last are those that acknowledge both sides—the necessity of control and the cost of it. What follows is not a chronicle of coins and credit but an anatomy of power, encoded in ledgers. By tracing how states invented money, we uncover the first protocol that made large-scale civilisation possible—and the logic that today's digital systems must confront or inherit. The code of money began as a story of kings; it may yet end as a story of networks.

From Tally Sticks to Seigniorage

In February 1834, a fire tore through the Palace of Westminster, consuming one of Britain's most curious archives: thousands of medieval tally sticks—split pieces of hazel wood once used to record tax obligations to the Crown. As flames leapt from the furnaces beneath the House of Lords, the smoke carried away six centuries of fiscal memory. These humble sticks, each marked with notches and names, had been more than accounting tools; they were physical embodiments of a political contract. A tally was worthless in isolation. Only when its two halves—the *stock* held by the Exchequer and the *foil* held by the taxpayer—matched could a debt be verified as paid. In that symmetry lay an early form of consensus, secured not by trust in the individual but by trust in the institution. The tally system's destruction was symbolic: by the nineteenth century, Britain had moved from wooden ledgers to paper credit, and from sovereign debt to a centralised financial system that owed its stability to the state's monopoly over money itself. The fire merely cremated an old protocol.

Money, from its inception, was never simply a medium of exchange; it was a means by which authority rendered itself visible. The medieval coin did not acquire legitimacy because it contained silver, but because it bore the monarch's face and sanction. Each coin was a condensed act of governance: the sovereign guaranteed weight, purity, and—most importantly—acceptance. To pay taxes, one had to use the ruler's currency; to pay wages, one had to trust that others would do the same. Thus coinage, ledger, and taxation formed a self-reinforcing circuit—value created by decree, circulated by necessity, and reclaimed through obligation. This loop established the first scalable monetary architecture: not an economy of barter replaced by convenience, but an economy of rule codified through currency.

Seigniorage, the profit derived by issuing money above its cost of production, turned that architecture into a source of power. In fourteenth-century France, King Philip IV debased the silver *denier tournois* to fund his wars against Flanders and England. The intrinsic metal content fell; the face value stayed. By 1306, Philip had extracted enormous fiscal gain, but at the price of public trust. Bread riots broke out in Paris. Yet the king's position survived because he alone could define legality of tender. That prerogative—the right to decide what counts as money—proved more durable than any minting metal. In modern form, seigniorage persists through central bank balance sheets: governments issue liabilities to acquire real resources. The methods differ—printing, borrowing, inflating—but the logic remains unchanged. Control over issuance is control over survival.

The persistence of this logic explains why states defend their monetary privileges with such intensity. When the English Parliament established the Bank of England in 1694, it was not merely founding a financial intermediary but institutionalising a partner in fiscal sovereignty. The Bank's power to issue notes in exchange for lending to the Crown bound public debt and public trust into a single feedback loop. Each war bond financed empire and entrenched the pound's authority. By the nineteenth century, as historian Niall Ferguson observed in *The Ascent of Money* (2008), the national debt had become the backbone of Britain's global dominance. Money was the bloodstream of governance—circulating power through credit rather than conquest.

This transformation was mirrored elsewhere. The Ming dynasty in China, which issued the *Da Ming Baochao* paper notes in the late fourteenth century, achieved a comparable centralisation of fiscal control. The notes promised value but were backed only by the state's command. When over-issuance led to hyperinflation, the government outlawed private exchange in silver to maintain the fiction of its monopoly. The result was predictable: public rejection, underground trade, and the slow decay of imperial authority. The Ming experiment exposed a recurring truth—when monetary systems lose the confidence of those compelled to use them, coercion can delay collapse but cannot prevent it. Legitimacy, not material, anchors value.

Money's essence, then, lies not in its physical form but in its institutional design. Whether encoded in tally sticks or blockchain ledgers, the crucial feature is the closure of the loop: issuance, circulation, redemption. In pre-modern economies, that loop was anchored by taxation. In digital systems, it is enforced by consensus algorithms and transaction fees. Both structures depend on rules that participants must trust yet cannot easily alter. A well-designed monetary protocol, whether administered by a treasury or a network, thus balances two imperatives: *credibility*—the promise that rules will hold—and *elasticity*—the capacity to adapt under stress. The history of state money is a chronicle of that balance tilting back and forth.

One might be tempted to imagine money's evolution as a steady march toward abstraction: from metal to paper to bits. Yet abstraction has always been political. The Roman Empire's denarius began as silver, but by the third century AD had become largely symbolic, its value sustained by the empire's administrative reach rather than its metallic worth. When confidence in imperial institutions eroded, so did the coin. Trust, not metal, was the scarce resource. That same truth re-emerged in the Renaissance, when Florentine bankers like the Medici turned bookkeeping into an art of persuasion. Their double-entry ledgers—meticulously recording credit and debit—became instruments of faith in numbers rather than persons. The ledger replaced the sword as the guarantor of continuity.

Seen from this lineage, modern cryptocurrencies represent not an unprecedented rupture but a re-enactment of an ancient tension: who commands the ledger, and who must trust it? Bitcoin's invention in 2009 offered a technical answer—replace institutional authority with algorithmic consensus—but the political question lingers. States view such systems not as toys but as threats precisely because they replicate the core functions of money—issuance, record-keeping, taxation-by-fee—outside sovereign control. To a central banker, the blockchain is not new technology; it is a rival protocol, audaciously proposing to coordinate value without hierarchy. That rivalry is constitutional, not commercial.

To see why, consider seigniorage in its digital form. In proof-of-work networks, miners create new currency units as rewards for securing the system, just as monarchs once extracted profit from minting coins. The analogy is imperfect but instructive: both regimes fund security through issuance. Yet whereas seigniorage once enriched rulers, in decentralised systems it subsidises infrastructure. The "senior claim" is distributed across a network of participants rather than centralised in a throne or treasury. This design diffuses power, but it also redistributes risk. When block rewards decline, as they will in Bitcoin's emission schedule, the system must transition from inflationary subsidy to fee-based security—a fiscal dilemma familiar to any state facing declining tax revenue. Governance, it seems, is an unavoidable layer of monetary design, no matter how cryptographic the architecture.

The counter-example, illuminating by contrast, lies in societies that attempted money without a coordinating sovereign. The Yapese stone money of Micronesia—giant limestone discs used for centuries as units of value—worked precisely because the island's small population shared an oral ledger of ownership. The stones never moved; their value was maintained by collective memory. Scale, however, was the limit. Once population or geography expanded, the system fractured. Without central authority or algorithmic enforcement, consensus decayed. That fragility underscores the paradox that haunts all monetary systems: decentralisation ensures resilience but limits scale; centralisation ensures scale but invites abuse. Every innovation must choose its failure mode.

The tally stick, the gold sovereign, the printed note, the blockchain—all are chapters in the same story: humanity's effort to formalise trust through record and rule. The transition from tally sticks to sovereign minting was not a technological upgrade but a constitutional consolidation. It brought efficiency and stability, but also hierarchy. As commerce globalised, the loop between money and state tightened further. Taxation no longer merely collected funds; it disciplined subjects into accepting the state's unit of account. When citizens paid in pounds or francs, they reaffirmed allegiance as much as obligation. Money became a civic language—one that bound communities more effectively than flags or creeds.

And yet, history's most enduring currencies are those that kept their promises believable without being brittle. The British pound survived wars and depressions because it could stretch its rules—suspend gold convertibility, adjust reserves, absorb colonies—without shattering confidence. The same elasticity now underwrites the fiat systems of the twenty-first century. But elasticity carries a hidden cost: opacity. As monetary instruments became digital, their mechanics receded from public view. Few citizens can now trace how central bank money is created, allocated, or destroyed. In that vacuum of understanding, blockchains claim legitimacy by offering transparency in place of trust. Whether they succeed depends on whether transparency can substitute for sovereignty.

If the fire of 1834 marked the end of one ledger, it also foreshadowed another. The Palace of Westminster was rebuilt as a gothic monument to parliamentary power, while the Bank of England—only a short walk away—quietly perfected the art of creating money from debt. The tally sticks, incinerated as relics, had already fulfilled their purpose: they demonstrated that the strength of a monetary system lies not in its materials but in its institutions. Today's digital protocols face the same test. They must close their own loops of value, obligation, and authority without reverting to the hierarchies they seek to escape.

The question, then, is not whether code can replace kings, but whether code can command belief with the same endurance. A tally stick held power because it reconciled two halves of trust; a blockchain must do the same, binding mathematics to human confidence. The first protocol was written in wood and sanctioned by the Crown. The next may be written in code and sanctioned by consensus. Both serve the same purpose: to make promises that a society can live by, and to decide who gets to keep them.

Credit, Trust, and the Myth of Metal

On 26 April 1478, in Florence, Lorenzo de' Medici authorised a transfer in his bank's ledger that settled a shipment of English wool without a single florin changing hands. The books recorded credits due from London and debits owed in Bruges; a clerk in the Medici *casa* balanced them with a few careful entries, and the merchant walked away satisfied. No chest, no gold, no guards. The transaction cleared because reputations matched and accounts aligned. The coin was incidental; the credit relationship was decisive. The coin looked strong; the entry made it final. The coin felt safe enough.

The scene unsettles the modern myth that metal made money safe. What carried authority in Renaissance finance was a social machine: names, dates, bills of exchange, and a network whose members cared about staying in the network. The Medici were not moving bullion across the Alps every week; they were matching claims, offsetting obligations, and netting positions so that a promise in Bruges discharged a debt in Florence. This was settlement without metal, but not without discipline. The discipline came from ledgers that could shame liars, and from courts that could ruin them. Weight did not create finality; enforceable recognition did.

Show the practice; name the institution; explain the mechanism; map the consequence. Florence, 1478, gives us our first demonstration that money is a grammar of promises before it is a catalogue of substances. The ledger does not deny the role of gold; it demotes it. Metal can anchor a price. It cannot, by itself, consummate a relationship. When a bill of exchange matured at a fair in Lyon, the payee cared that the drawer's signature would be honoured by a house with a reputation to lose. That is finality as behaviour: a clerk stamping *pagato*, a courier instructed, a daybook closed.

Now consider Amsterdam in 1609. The city's magistrates founded the Wisselbank—the Bank of Amsterdam—to discipline chaotic coinage and standardise payments. Merchants deposited a ragbag of clipped and debased coins and received *bank money*, a unit more trusted than any particular metal piece then in circulation. The bank did not lend; it merely kept accounts and settled transfers by adjusting balances. Here was hardness without gold's glamour. The finality lay in the *giro*, the book entry that could not be undone without the bank's consent. The key metric was not karats but a spread: the premium at which *bank money* traded over loose coin on the market. When that premium widened, confidence rose; when it narrowed, doubts crept in. The implication is clear: an institution can make a ledger "harder" than metal by making reversals costly and reputational stakes high. The measure is the price of access to that ledger, not the glint of its reserves.

A second example, equally checkable, sits across the Channel. In 1797, under pressure from war with France, the Bank of England suspended specie payments—the Restriction Period. Banknotes no longer converted to gold on demand. Yet commerce continued. Wages were paid, contracts honoured, debts enforced. The Crown's courts still treated the pound as settlement if the Bank's notes were tendered. The visible behaviour was mundane: shopkeepers posted prices in paper; tax collectors accepted the same. The explanation is not alchemy but architecture. The Bank's liabilities were supported by tax capacity and legal privilege; the state had both the will and the means to treat paper as final. The implication is unsettling for metallic faith: convertibility can sustain confidence, but the power to name what discharges a debt can replace convertibility when required. Metal can be a promise's ritual; the law makes it binding.

These cases help separate two ideas often conflated: *settlement finality* and *perceived hardness*. Finality is an institutional act. It is the moment a system declares, "This obligation is over." In Renaissance Italy, finality was the acceptance of a bill by a reputable house and the entry that balanced accounts. In Amsterdam, it was the *giro* at the Wisselbank, overseen by magistrates who had stakes in the city's trade. In London, it was the Bank's note backed by tax capacity and legal privilege. Hardness, by contrast, is a property we attribute to media we think cannot be easily altered—gold bars with a hallmark,

coins with a fixed weight, or, in our time, protocols with predetermined issuance schedules. Hardness reassures. Finality frees. We should not confuse the comfort of holding something heavy with the certainty that a chain of obligations has ended.

Metal has its own undeniable virtue: its resistance to arbitrary multiplication. The Spanish *real de a ocho*, minted from New World silver and circulating from Manila to Madrid in the seventeenth and eighteenth centuries, gained global acceptance because its weight and purity were broadly reliable. Prices in Canton and Veracruz quoted in the same coin because the coin's content could be tested by touchstone and scale. Here, perception matched material. This was the myth at its strongest, and for good reasons. A merchant in Manila could shave minutes off a bargain by trusting the sound of a coin on a counter rather than a stranger's paper. The visible behaviour—biting a coin, weighing it, listening for a clear ring—was a test of metal that stood in for a test of character. The implication is that metal reduces some costs of verification, especially at the boundaries of trust.

Yet even the silver dollar owed its reach to institutions: mints enforcing standards, courts punishing counterfeiters, and empires protecting shipping lanes. When the flow of bullion faltered or debasement crept in, the coin's "hardness" could not save its purchasing power. The counter-example that proves the point is instructive: during the California Gold Rush in 1849, gold dust circulated as payment in mining camps, but only after assayers certified quality. Without assay, dust was a quarrel in a pouch. With assay, dust became contract. The dust did not settle debts; the certificate did. Reconciling this with the myth requires humility. Metal helps when institutions are weak or distant, but it cannot substitute for them at scale. The ledger is the final court.

The motif that guides this subchapter is simple: *The ring on the counter.* Imagine the sound of a coin striking wood, the audible claim "I am what I say." Now pair it with the quiet scratch of a clerk's quill entering a counterparty's name beside an amount and a date. Which sound closes the obligation? The ring seduces; the scratch decides. We return to this question because it trains the ear for neutrality claims in crypto. When a blockchain advertises "hardness" through a halving schedule or fixed cap, it offers the ring. When it guarantees settlement through consensus finality and costly reorganisation, it offers the scratch. The two can align. They can also diverge.

Renaissance banking clarifies the social engine that made scratches authoritative. Merchants managed risk by running *acceptance* networks: a bill bearing the endorsement of a house like the Medici or the Fuggers could be discounted in Antwerp at a lower rate than a bill drawn by a lesser-known trader. The metric was the discount rate, visible on the street. The behaviour was decisive: pay 99 now for 100 due in sixty days if the signer's name is good; demand 97 if it is not. Naming the mechanism—acceptance and discount—explains why credit outran metal. In a market where reputations carried prices, character became collateral. The implication is direct for any claim of neutrality: what counts as "neutral" depends on whose name the system already trusts.

Gold regimes were not immune to the pull of credit. Isaac Newton, as Master of the Mint, fixed the guinea at 21 shillings in 1717, nudging Britain towards a gold standard well before formal adoption. Yet even under gold rules, the nineteenth-century City of London ran on bills, acceptances, and the Bank of England's *lender of last resort* commitment. Walter Bagehot described the remedy in 1873: lend freely, at a high rate, to sound institutions against good collateral. The visible behaviour in crises—the Bank extending discount, the discount houses queuing—shows that settlement finality rested on an elastic promise from a discretionary actor. Gold in the vault reassured savers. A central bank in the room saved the system. The implication for hardness is uncomfortable: the very survivability of "hard" money regimes depended on discretionary, social credit at decisive moments.

A credible counter-argument maintains that metal constrains political abuse. It can. The pre-1914 classical gold standard restrained fiscal adventurism by forcing countries to defend parity. When outflows depleted reserves, governments raised discount rates, cut spending, or endured recession. This discipline had metrics: gold reserves as a ratio to notes, the Bank Rate posted weekly, the current account. It also had costs: unemployment spikes, deflationary pressure, and, at times, a bias against domestic welfare.

Reconciling the constraint with our thesis yields a hard lesson: metal can discipline the sovereign, but it does so by outsourcing domestic pain to maintain external credibility. Finality for creditors often meant instability for workers. The ring was clear; the scratch scarred.

The twentieth century's breaks made these trade-offs visible. In March 1933, Franklin Roosevelt suspended gold convertibility for Americans and later revalued gold at $35 per ounce. Contracts denominated in gold clauses were voided by Congress and upheld by the Supreme Court in 1935. The behaviour is stark: judges ruled that a promise to pay in gold was now satisfied by paper at the new rate. Finality moved from assay to statute. The implication is that even the hardest clauses yield to the highest court. Hardness cannot bind a polity that decides otherwise.

What, then, prepares us to evaluate crypto claims about neutrality? First, listen for the ring and the scratch. When advocates praise a fixed supply, they evoke metal's aura: predictable issuance. Ask for the corresponding mechanism that declares a transaction irreversibly settled and measures the cost of rewriting history. In proof-of-work systems, that cost is energy burned and hash rate deployed; in proof-of-stake, it is stake at risk and slashing enforced. These are visible metrics, not metaphysics: exahashes per second, percentage of stake bonded, time to probabilistic finality, depth of reorganisation feasible at current security budgets. The behaviour is equally concrete: exchanges wait a set number of confirmations before crediting deposits; users pay higher fees to prioritise inclusion in the next block. Neutrality must be audible in such practices.

Second, examine whose names the system already trusts. Even in decentralised networks, core software clients, major validators or miners, and dominant exchanges play gatekeeping roles. They publish updates; they adopt or refuse forks; they whitelist or pause assets under regulatory pressure. When Ethereum executed the DAO hard fork in July 2016 to reverse an exploit, the community asserted a value—social recovery of misallocated funds—over strict ledger immutability. A neutralist might object; a pragmatist might cheer. The fact to record is the behaviour: the fork happened, clients adopted it, markets priced the decision. The implication is not that blockchains lack neutrality, but that their neutrality is a negotiated property, reasserted at every constitutional moment.

Third, separate settlement from spectacle. A transfer that appears quickly on a block explorer is not final until the chain's consensus deems it costly to reverse. In Bitcoin, that is often heuristically measured by six confirmations; in Ethereum post-Merge (09/2022), *finality* is marked at the consensus layer after two epochs under normal conditions. These are not theological numbers; they are operational choices balancing security and speed. The visible decisions—how many confirmations an exchange requires, how long a merchant waits—give the lie to purity myths. Neutrality is lived as waiting, not proclaimed as principle.

Return to the motif. The ring seduces. A fixed cap or halving schedule makes a clean sound. But the scratch decides. Rules for client updates, quorum for upgrades, thresholds for slashing, and governance around parameter changes compose the handwriting that endows a ledger with finality. Weight impresses; process binds. When a protocol claims "credible neutrality," read its process. Who drafts EIPs? Who merges code? Who can credibly veto a fork by refusing to upgrade? The metrics may be prosaic—GitHub commit histories, client diversity statistics, validator concentration by geography—but they map the distance between aspiration and practice.

A final look at the gold myth reveals its core seduction: the hope that value can be anchored outside politics. Gold felt like a vote of no confidence in human discretion. But politics did not disappear; it migrated. It determined mint standards, legal tender laws, convertibility rules, and suspension procedures. Crypto replicates the pattern. Politics moves into code repositories, governance forums, and the business models of exchanges and custodians. The site of discretion changes; the fact of discretion remains. The test for neutrality is not the absence of politics but its domestication: are the processes legible, predictable, and open to exit?

The unresolved tension should remain unresolved. If money is social credit, metal cannot redeem us from each other. If settlement finality is institutional, code cannot redeem us from politics. What, then, do we prefer: a ring that constrains rulers by external discipline, or a scratch that binds communities by transparent process? Or a composite architecture that admits both? Before accepting any claim of neutrality—golden, algorithmic, or constitutional—ask a clerk's question: who writes *paid* in the book, and at what cost could they be persuaded to erase it?

Crisis as Feature: Why States Break Their Own Rules

On 3 September 1939, as Britain declared war on Germany, the Chancellor of the Exchequer, Sir John Simon, authorised the immediate suspension of gold convertibility. The pound, once exchangeable for gold at the Bank of England, ceased to be so. The decision was made not through debate in Parliament but by administrative order—an act of monetary triage. Within hours, the state had broken one of its own sacred promises: that the currency could be redeemed in metal. Yet markets stabilised, not collapsed. The Bank's vaults still held gold, but its convertibility had become irrelevant; what mattered was that the government could finance war. The rule had been abandoned to preserve the regime that had written it.

Crisis exposes money's hidden constitution. Every rule of issuance, convertibility, and debt management is a compromise between credibility and flexibility. The gold standard offered credibility through constraint—an iron rule that forbade inflationary temptation—but its rigidity was fatal when nations faced existential shocks. Elasticity, by contrast, allows survival but invites discretion, discretion breeds suspicion, and suspicion erodes faith. States must therefore oscillate between two unlovely options: brittle integrity or adaptive deceit. The pattern is older than modern finance, older even than central banks. When power is measured in the capacity to pay, rule-bending becomes not an aberration but a survival trait.

The recurring motif here is the *elastic ledger.* It stretches in crisis and contracts in calm. How far it can stretch without tearing measures a society's resilience. Consider two emblematic episodes. The first: Britain's suspension of the gold standard in 1797, amid the Napoleonic wars. The second: Franklin Roosevelt's banking holiday and gold confiscation in 1933. Both reveal the same logic—rules give way to preserve the authority behind them. In February 1797, as rumours spread of a French invasion, panic-stricken depositors besieged the Bank of England. To prevent collapse, Prime Minister William Pitt the Younger issued the Restriction Act, allowing the Bank to refuse specie payments. Paper money—backed only by state decree—became legal tender. Pitt's decision violated orthodoxy but saved solvency. When convertibility resumed in 1821, the pound's credibility had endured, not evaporated. The rule's suspension had reaffirmed the state's ability to defend its fiscal core.

Now jump forward to 1933, Washington D.C. The Great Depression had gutted confidence; banks failed daily. On 6 March, Roosevelt declared a four-day national banking holiday, froze withdrawals, and prohibited the hoarding of gold. Within weeks, the Gold Reserve Act expropriated private holdings and revalued gold upward from $20.67 to $35 per ounce—a 69 percent devaluation of the dollar's metal parity. It was a constitutional shock, executed by executive order. Yet the public did not revolt; confidence returned. Deposits flowed back. The federal government had reasserted control over liquidity by rewriting its own contract. The rule-break became the remedy.

These are not aberrations. They are features of a system built to survive exogenous shock. Money, when institutionalised by states, must trade predictability for persistence. Each suspension, confiscation, or inflation is an implicit confession: rules are instruments, not absolutes. What separates collapse from adaptation is the narrative that justifies the exception. In 1797 and 1933 alike, rule-breaking was framed not as fraud but as necessity, an emergency measure to protect the larger promise of order. Credibility re-emerged from elasticity.

Elasticity, however, breeds moral hazard. Once the state proves it can rewrite its monetary constitution, restraint becomes optional. The twentieth century is a study in this tension. The post-war Bretton Woods system (1944) restored a version of gold convertibility—$35 to the ounce—but only for central banks. Private citizens remained bound to fiat. For a quarter-century, the system projected stability while practising selective flexibility. Capital controls muffled the noise; deficits were tolerated as long as they served reconstruction. But by August 1971, when Richard Nixon closed the "gold window," the pretence collapsed. America's reserves could no longer support the claims made upon them. The global dollar, unanchored, survived. The gold standard's death was not a failure of policy; it was the final proof that rigidity cannot govern an industrial democracy at scale. Nixon's televised declaration—"Your dollar will be worth just as much tomorrow as it is today"—was the most famous lie ever told to defend a currency. Yet it worked.

The elasticity of state money is mirrored in the mechanisms through which states raise it. War is the original engine of fiscal innovation. The Napoleonic conflicts birthed the first mass bond markets. The First World War normalised deficit financing on a continental scale. Between 1914 and 1918, Britain's national debt ballooned from £650 million to over £7 billion, funded largely by War Loan bonds marketed as patriotic duty. Posters promised safety and victory; inflation did the rest. The "price" of survival was the slow debasement of purchasing power. Predictability was sacrificed so that the state could command men and resources beyond its immediate means. Every conscription of soldiers was mirrored by the conscription of savings.

The 2008 financial crisis replayed the pattern in digital form. When Lehman Brothers collapsed in September that year, governments and central banks broke their own doctrines of non-intervention. The U.S. Treasury guaranteed money-market funds; the Federal Reserve bought mortgage-backed securities; the Bank of England launched quantitative easing in March 2009, injecting £75 billion into the economy. Each measure blurred boundaries between fiscal and monetary power, between prudence and improvisation. The metrics—balance sheet size, interest rate floor, debt-to-GDP ratio—became abstractions of expediency. Yet the system endured. Rules had bent, but the ledger held.

Crises clarify priorities. In 2020, as the COVID-19 pandemic froze global commerce, even the most orthodox regimes suspended fiscal restraint. The European Union temporarily lifted its Stability and Growth Pact limits; the United States issued stimulus payments totalling over $800 billion; the Bank of Japan directly financed government bonds. The shared behaviour was decisive: *print, distribute, stabilise.* The old fear of inflation yielded to the immediate fear of collapse. Elasticity became policy. The longer-term cost—distorted asset prices, widened inequality, political backlash—was deferred, as it always is. The ledger stretched again.

The counter-example most often cited is the Weimar Republic's hyperinflation (1921–23), where elasticity tore the ledger beyond repair. Paper marks multiplied; prices doubled daily; wages were paid in wheelbarrows. Here, rule-breaking metastasised into disintegration. Yet even Weimar's collapse confirms the same law: when elasticity loses its narrative anchor—when citizens no longer believe the state can restore constraint—the monetary order ceases to function. Hyperinflation was not caused by printing alone but by the loss of fiscal credibility after the punitive Treaty of Versailles. Elasticity without narrative becomes chaos; narrative without elasticity becomes tyranny.

A more recent cautionary case is Greece during the eurozone crisis of 2010–15. Bound by the European Central Bank's rules and unable to devalue its currency, Athens endured austerity of medieval severity: GDP contracted by 25 percent, unemployment exceeded 27 percent, public services disintegrated. The euro's rigidity made predictability absolute but resilience impossible. Greece's suffering demonstrated the opposite failure mode: when rules cannot bend, societies break. The lesson, whether drawn from Weimar's elasticity or Europe's austerity, is that legitimacy—not discipline—is money's ultimate collateral.

The motif of the *elastic ledger* returns. States stretch it by borrowing, by inflating, by suspending convertibility, or by rewriting contracts. Each stretch carries a cost. Too much elasticity and the currency frays into distrust; too little and it snaps under stress. The state's art lies in timing the stretch—how far, how fast, and with what justification. In that calibration lies sovereignty itself.

What does this tell us about the digital contenders now claiming to replace state money? Cryptocurrencies, by design, are brittle. Their protocols hard-code scarcity, fix issuance schedules, and outlaw discretion. Bitcoin's supply halving every 210,000 blocks is the antithesis of fiscal elasticity; its governance culture treats any change as heresy. That rigidity is its moral appeal and its strategic vulnerability. During shocks—price crashes, exchange hacks, network congestion—the protocol cannot intervene. There is no equivalent of Pitt's Restriction Act or Roosevelt's gold decree. In 2020, when oil futures briefly traded negative, governments stabilised markets. When crypto markets collapsed that same year, the networks simply recorded it. Algorithmic discipline survived; human users paid the price.

Ethereum, more flexible by design, illustrates the alternative. After the 2016 DAO exploit drained 3.6 million ether, its developers initiated a hard fork to reverse the theft—effectively rewriting history. It was a microcosm of state elasticity: rules bent to preserve the system's legitimacy. The fork restored confidence for most users, but it fractured the community, birthing Ethereum Classic as the faction of purists who refused to accept rule-breaking. The motif replays itself: brittle integrity versus adaptive discretion, now expressed in code.

Elasticity is therefore not a monopoly of states but a property of governance under pressure. What distinguishes the state is its ability to externalise costs across society. When central banks expand balance sheets, they tax holders of money through inflation. When crypto networks socialise losses, they do so through forks or implicit dilution. Both systems shift pain to preserve continuity. Both depend on belief that the mechanism—monetary or algorithmic—serves a larger order worth saving.

The paradox is that each generation condemns the last for its flexibility while relying on it for its inheritance. Without the 1797 suspension, Britain might have lost its wars; without Roosevelt's devaluation, the U.S. might have lost its banks; without quantitative easing, the 2008 collapse might have metastasised into depression. The moral judgement—"rule-breaking"—misunderstands the function. Elasticity is the mechanism through which systems reboot under duress. Predictability builds trust in calm; discretion preserves it in crisis. A sound architecture requires both.

The unresolved tension endures. Should money be governed by immutable code or adaptable conscience? Should societies pre-commit to rules they cannot change or trust in rulers who can? The *elastic ledger* waits for its next test. When the next shock comes—pandemic, cyberwar, or climate crisis—somebody, somewhere, will again reach for the emergency key and rewrite the rules. The only real variable is how convincingly they will say it was for our own good.

What Money Measures: Power, Promises, Permissions

On 8 November 2016 in New Delhi, Prime Minister Narendra Modi announced that India's ₹500 and ₹1,000 banknotes would cease to be legal tender at midnight. Queues formed at ATMs; shopkeepers taped handwritten signs to their shutters; bank clerks counted and re-counted deposits while television anchors read the decree on loop. A government spoke and, by speaking, changed the unit that discharged debts. No vaults moved. The ledger moved. A single decision revealed three levers at once: who may issue and cancel money (power), what rules bind its value and convertibility (promises), and who may access and use it without impediment (permissions). Turn one lever and the others shift. Turn all three and society jolts. Five words summarise the demonstration: authority edits the payments script.

This is the diagnostic schema that will guide the chapter: *Power, Promises, Permissions*. Each axis can be measured by visible behaviours rather than slogans. Power is who sets issuance and can credibly revise it—minutes of rate-setting committees, emergency decrees, signatures on new notes. Promises are the explicit rules—convertibility clauses, inflation targets, fee schedules, consensus thresholds—and the discipline to honour them when tempted not to. Permissions are the access rules—KYC checks, withdrawal caps, whitelists, blacklists, network fees, app interfaces. Most debates about "sound money" collapse these axes into a single moral preference. Most failures occur because the axes were misread, or their interactions ignored.

The first claim is simple: money is an institution whose power concentrates around issuance. Show this concentration; name a specific case; explain the mechanism; draw the implication. London, 1694: the Bank of England received its royal charter and began issuing notes in exchange for lending to the Crown. With that charter, the state outsourced its balance sheet while keeping the constitutional core—defining legal tender and tax obligations. The Bank's directors set issuance in line with the Treasury's needs, and Parliament endorsed the arrangement by accepting the Bank's money in taxes. Power thus sat with a small circle whose meetings produced concrete outputs—note plates, discount rates, gilt auctions. The implication is not conspiratorial; it is structural. Issuance power tends to centralise because someone must decide when public promises meet private balance sheets. You can read it in the minutes.

Our second claim follows: promises are rules about value, not decorations on paper. They are costly to break in calm and tempting to break in crisis. Consider Washington, August 1971. Facing dwindling gold reserves and persistent deficits, President Richard Nixon closed the "gold window", ending dollar convertibility at $35 per ounce. The outcome was immediate: the Bretton Woods parity system unravelled; the dollar floated. The visible behaviour was prosaic—banks repriced contracts; importers changed invoices; central banks stopped shipping bullion. The promise that had anchored a generation was revised by decree. The deeper explanation is that promises implicitly trade off with power: binding convertibility constrains issuance, and constrained issuance limits the state's capacity to respond to shocks. The implication is normative only in the sense that societies must choose their constraints. If the promise is sacred, the power is narrow. If the power is wide, the promise is conditional.

The third claim completes the triangle: permissions are the politics of daily life. Who may hold, move, exchange, and save in a given unit? Who may not? Show, name, explain, imply. Nairobi, March 2007: Safaricom launched M-Pesa, a mobile money service that allowed users to store value and transfer it by SMS. No bank account required. Within a year, millions of Kenyans paid bills, wages, and school fees through their phones. The decisive metric was not an interest rate but a map: the density of cash-in/cash-out agents. Every added kiosk widened permissions. The implication could be seen in matatu fares and market stalls: monetary design allocates dignity and time. Where access expands, informal economies formalise. Where access narrows, people queue.

Introduce the motif: *three dials*. Turn the issuance dial and strain the others; turn the promise dial and restrict manoeuvre; turn the permission dial and alter social order. The dials travel together even when policymakers claim otherwise. The pattern reappears across centuries.

Amsterdam, 1609, gives our first composite example. The city's magistrates founded the Wisselbank to eliminate the confusion of debased coins and foreign moneys. Merchants deposited irregular coin and received balances in "bank money," transferred by book entry. Power was municipal and tightly held: the city appointed governors and audited reserves. Promises were spartan but steel-edged: balances would be paid out at a fixed ratio to good coin, and the bank would not lend against its deposits. Permissions widened inside the city walls because *giro* transfers were cheap and final. The observable metric was the *agio*—the premium at which bank money traded over loose coin. When the agio rose, merchants preferred the bank's ledger; when it fell, confidence faltered. Over time, the Wisselbank drifted from its promise by secretly lending to the Dutch East India Company. The agio told the truth before the minutes did. Turn the power dial in the back room and the promise dial moves on the trading floor.

A second example, modern and measurable, shows how a single sentence can pull all three dials at once. On 26 July 2012 in London, European Central Bank President Mario Draghi said the ECB was ready to do "whatever it takes" to preserve the euro. Yields on Spanish and Italian government bonds fell within days; the Outright Monetary Transactions programme was later designed to back the pledge. Power shifted toward the ECB's Governing Council, which now held a conditional right to purchase sovereign debt. The promise was informal at first—a phrase in a speech—but it hardened into a policy framework with eligibility criteria. Permissions expanded implicitly for eurozone citizens: access to functioning payments and state salaries no longer depended on the bond market's mood each week. The visible behaviours were price moves and documents: ten-year spreads compressing; an ECB press release describing sterilisation and conditionality. The implication is instructive: sometimes a promise is credible because power stands ready behind it, even before the legal drafting catches up.

A credible counter-example tempers the schema's optimism. The eurozone crisis also produced a restriction that illustrates the tyranny of a promise when it binds the wrong thing. Athens, 2015: capital controls limited cash withdrawals and cross-border transfers as the Greek state negotiated with its creditors. Here, the promise that the euro would be irrevocable within the monetary union collided with the politics of adjustment. Greece lacked issuance power; the promise constrained fiscal choices; permissions narrowed overnight. The visible behaviours were demeaning and precise: daily ATM caps, card acceptance refused at fuel stations, pensioners turned away from banks. The diagnosis is not that promises are bad, but that promises without local power force permissions to do the dirty work. The reconciliation is honest rather than easy: a currency designed to integrate economies must decide whether the power dial sits in Frankfurt, in capitals, or in a rulebook that can be suspended without humiliation.

Now apply the schema to stateless money. Bitcoin distributes issuance by algorithm, sets promises in code (fixed supply, predictable halving), and maximises permissions at the network edge (no identity required to validate or transact). The behaviours are measurable: blocks every roughly ten minutes; supply declining on a known schedule; the cost to reorganise N blocks at current hash rate; the confirmation thresholds that exchanges require before crediting deposits. The implication is double-edged. High promise discipline and wide permissions grant censorship resistance, but low discretionary power removes the ability to respond to shocks. When fees spike during congestion, permissions narrow de facto because poorer users are priced out. The dial turns itself. To widen permissions again, the system must either rely on off-chain arrangements—custodial wallets, lightning channels, wrapped tokens—or accept changes that adjust fee markets or blockspace, which are forms of power creeping back through the side door.

Ethereum locates its dials differently. Its issuance power is more flexible, exercised through social consensus that accepts frequent client updates; its promises emphasise computation and upgradability rather than supply alone; its permissions mix openness with protocol-level complexity that shifts risk to the application layer. We can see the dials move in public. The 2016 DAO fork demonstrated discretionary power; the 2022 Merge redefined promises about energy use and finality; the rise of liquid staking has concentrated permissions in large providers, measured by their share of validator keys and client diversity statistics. These are not "gotchas". They are diagnostics. A system that promises expressive computation will naturally accumulate governance questions at the edges. The implication is straightforward: when reading neutrality claims, inspect the dials, not the manifesto.

Bring the schema back to states with current instruments. Central Bank Digital Currencies (CBDCs) allow governments to set the dials with more granularity than banknotes ever permitted. Issuance power becomes programmable (helicopter money with time limits), promises acquire conditionality (negative rates, smart compliance), and permissions can be tuned per-transaction (whitelists for aid, blacklists for sanctioned entities). The behaviours are not speculative; pilot projects already test them. China's e-CNY trials have distributed digital wallets with spending cups and expiry features; the Bahamas' Sand Dollar has mapped offline payments to hurricane preparedness. The implication is profound: architecture encodes ideology. A retail CBDC that mandates identity for all transactions tightens the permission dial while keeping power wide and promises flexible. A wholesale CBDC restricted to banks does the opposite. The dials tell you how liberty will feel at the counter.

The schema is also useful for reading stablecoins. A fully reserved dollar token issued by a regulated trust company concentrates power in its issuer (reserve management, blacklist controls), makes a simple promise (redeem at par on demand), and sets permissions with API keys and compliance programmes. The behaviours are empirical: attestations of reserves by named auditors; public blacklisting events recorded on-chain; redemption volumes during stress. Move any dial and the profile changes. Relax permissions by allowing pseudonymous wallets and the issuer attracts regulators; tighten them and users migrate to alternatives with weaker promises or riskier power. An algorithmic stablecoin, by contrast, decentralises power among arbitrageurs and governance token holders, promises parity via incentives rather than assets, and often widens permissions by design. The implication is cautionary: when promises rely on reflexivity rather than collateral, the permission dial can stay wide only while confidence—the least durable reserve—holds.

The motif of the three dials bears one final pass because it disciplines analysis. Start with issuance: who writes the numbers into existence, and what minutes, code commits, or decrees evidence that control? Then promises: what is the contract—explicit or algorithmic—that regulates inflation, convertibility, fees, or finality, and how has it behaved under stress? Last, permissions: what does a user need to move value—an ID card, a node, an app—and who can say no? Each question yields a behaviour, a metric, a document. Each answer implies a politics. A currency that maximises power and minimises permissions is efficient for rulers. One that maximises permissions and locks promises may be brittle in war. Most real systems sit between ideals, moving under pressure.

A counterpoint, and a useful one, is the Swiss WIR credit circle, founded in 1934. It is a complementary currency where small and medium businesses extend credit to one another in a closed network, debiting and crediting accounts without francs changing hands. Power is distributed across participants; promises are enforced by mutual surveillance and collateral arrangements; permissions are restricted to members. The behaviour is steady rather than spectacular: counter-cyclical trade within the network rises when bank credit tightens. The WIR does not scale to a national unit of account, but it buffers local economies. Reconciling this with our framework shows its breadth: systems with narrow permissions can still be democratic if power is dispersed and promises are credible. The dials can point inward and still serve dignity.

What does the schema ask of the reader? It asks you to stop asking whether a currency is "good" and start asking where its dials sit today and where they move under strain. A state that raises issuance to fight a war must either revise promises (inflation, devaluation) or narrow permissions (capital controls). A blockchain that ossifies promises must either tolerate exclusion when fees rise or reintroduce power through upgrades and off-chain layers. A stablecoin that widens permissions will face pressure to concentrate power in compliance teams. Each design reshapes risk and social order. Each design reveals its values at the counter.

The unresolved question should stay open. How far should a society pre-commit to rules that limit its future moves, and how far should it trust human hands to turn the dials when the sirens sound? The answer cannot be given once. It must be governed, measured, and revised—by ballots, by code reviews, by balance sheets, and by the quiet moral test of who waits longest in the queue.

Chapter 2
Bitcoin's Break: Credible Rules Without a Ruler

In January 2009, a message appeared inside a block of code: *"The Times 03/Jan/2009 Chancellor on brink of second bailout for banks."* It was a timestamp, a protest, and a declaration of design. Buried in Bitcoin's first block, this headline from *The Times* of London did more than mark the date of its creation—it framed the problem it was built to solve. Where governments and banks had fused into a cycle of risk and rescue, Bitcoin proposed a different covenant: rules that could not beg for exceptions, money whose credibility would not depend on those in office, and consensus secured not by decree but by mathematics. The software's pseudonymous author, Satoshi Nakamoto, offered a simple provocation in code form—*what if we could replace the trust we place in institutions with the trust we place in process?*

The experiment began small: a few computers, an obscure mailing list, and an idea so radical it seemed naïve. Yet within a decade, Bitcoin had matured from digital curiosity to monetary heresy. It built a functioning payment and settlement network without a central administrator, sustained by miners who expended electricity to prove honesty. Its promise was not speed or efficiency but *credibility*: transactions recorded in a ledger that could not easily be rewritten, and a money supply whose schedule was visible to all and negotiable by none. Every rule—issuance, validation, finality—was public, deterministic, and voluntary. But its very success in securing credibility raised the deeper question this chapter explores: can a system remain neutral, incorruptible, and leaderless once humans begin to rely on it?

Bitcoin's breakthrough was not technological alone; it was constitutional. By replacing centralised authority with *probabilistic finality*—a notion that consensus could emerge from competing proofs of computational work—it built a self-enforcing equilibrium. Each miner's incentive to play by the rules was grounded in cost: electricity and hardware, expended upfront. Proof-of-work thus served as both a gatekeeper and a referee. If an attacker wished to falsify the ledger, they would need to outspend the honest network itself. In that sense, Nakamoto's design was a bargain—one that traded throughput and energy efficiency for governance transparency. Transactions were slow and costly, but the process was legible, auditable, and fair by construction. Where fiat money derives legitimacy from law and force, Bitcoin derives it from thermodynamics and consensus probability. Every block mined is a vote cast for order against entropy.

Yet Bitcoin's most striking feature is not its cleverness but its restraint. Unlike almost every technological system that prizes innovation, Bitcoin prizes ossification. Its culture treats change as risk, not progress. Protocol upgrades require overwhelming social coordination and near-unanimous consent. When internal disputes arise—such as the 2017 block-size war—they are not settled by fiat but by *fork*. Competing visions simply diverge into separate chains, each carrying its own version of history. The metaphor is biological: mutation through schism. This deliberate resistance to change confers stability. Bitcoin's minimalism—its refusal to evolve quickly—functions as a defence mechanism. A system that moves slowly is harder to capture, easier to predict, and more trustworthy as a base layer for global value. Stillness becomes security.

This chapter follows those tensions closely. Bitcoin's conservatism is not philosophical nostalgia; it is the price of credible neutrality. Every new feature, every line of code added to increase usability or throughput, risks introducing discretion—the very quality the protocol was built to avoid. A payments network can optimise for speed or sovereignty, but not both. Visa's settlement finality depends on institutional reversibility; Bitcoin's depends on economic irreversibility. To alter the ledger is to rewire history. The network's immune response to change—its slow, public, and often painful decision-making—should therefore be read as an achievement, not a flaw. It has learned what every polity eventually learns: that the harder it is to change the rules, the less those rules depend on rulers.

Still, the system's apparent serenity conceals an unsolved problem. The same mechanism that secured Bitcoin's birth—the *block reward* paid to miners—decays over time. Every four years, the subsidy halves, forcing the network to rely more on transaction fees. This shift, sometimes called the *security budget dilemma*, will define Bitcoin's long-term survival. The incentive to maintain honesty—the expenditure of energy—must be compensated by a steady flow of fees, or miners will abandon the field. If demand falls, security weakens; if fees rise, usability suffers. A money that aspires to neutrality must continually finance its own incorruptibility. The question is not whether Bitcoin can persist, but whether it can pay for its credibility once its minting slows to zero. The halving is both a ritual of faith and a reminder of fragility.

Every discussion of Bitcoin's economics therefore conceals a deeper ethical wager. What, exactly, does Bitcoin optimise for? Its architecture sacrifices convenience for integrity, expressivity for predictability, and human governance for algorithmic austerity. It refuses the compromises of financial modernity—chargebacks, discretionary liquidity, elastic credit—in favour of hard limits and visible consequences. In moments of geopolitical tension, this rigidity has proven revelatory. When protesters in Lagos or Kyiv have found their bank accounts frozen, Bitcoin has offered a channel of value immune to censorship. When capital controls in Cyprus or Argentina trapped citizens' savings, the blockchain demonstrated an unsettling alternative: money without permission. But the same features that make it powerful also make it austere. A network that cannot censor cannot easily protect; a ledger that cannot lie cannot easily forgive.

The motif that will thread through this chapter is *the clock without a custodian.* Bitcoin's ledger advances in time, one block every ten minutes on average, indifferent to its users' desires. Its governance resembles the slow, mechanical tick of a watch whose gears are sealed against tampering. Yet even this clock depends on human agreement to keep winding it—to maintain nodes, to update software, to exchange electricity for cryptographic truth. The paradox is stark: a system built to transcend politics survives only through political discipline. Each upgrade proposal, each fork debate, is a miniature referendum on the limits of rule without rulers.

As we descend into the mechanics of proof-of-work, the economics of block subsidies, and the sociology of governance by code, one question will shadow every section: what does it mean for a society to trust a machine more than it trusts itself? Bitcoin's architecture is not an escape from human nature but a mirror held to it—a reminder that rules are credible only when enough people choose to obey them, even when disobedience is cheaper. This chapter, then, is not just about software. It is about a civilisational experiment in restraint, an audacious attempt to make trust measurable, and an open question about whether such a thing can endure once belief becomes expectation.

The clock is still ticking. The rules still hold. But who winds them, and for how long, remains the live question Bitcoin asks of the age.

The Nakamoto Bargain

On 12 January 2009, Satoshi Nakamoto sent ten bitcoins to Hal Finney, a cryptographer in California. The transaction, recorded in block 170 of the fledgling network, was the first peer-to-peer digital transfer of value without a bank, a company, or a state standing behind it. There was no intermediary, no permission, no clearing house—just code, computation, and consensus. Finney later described the moment with characteristic understatement: "Running bitcoin." Those two words marked a civilisational milestone: the first time strangers coordinated trust through proof of work rather than through an institution.

To grasp the magnitude of that moment, it helps to recall the financial winter from which it emerged. In October 2008, global interbank lending froze, trust between counterparties evaporated, and central banks flooded the world with liquidity to prevent collapse. "Trust," that most human of currencies, had become an accounting liability. Against this backdrop, Nakamoto's white paper proposed an unorthodox alternative—a payment system where verification replaced trust entirely. Instead of banks reconciling ledgers, Bitcoin's nodes would compete to solve cryptographic puzzles whose difficulty adjusted automatically to the network's collective power. Each successful miner would earn newly minted bitcoins and the right to append a block of transactions to the chain. This mechanism, *proof-of-work*, was less a technical hack than a governance design: it distributed authority through cost.

The bargain was audaciously simple. If participants were forced to expend real resources to validate history, their incentives would align with the system's integrity. Energy and computation became the entry ticket to legitimacy. Nakamoto had inverted a thousand years of monetary logic. Where previous systems built trust by centralising it—banks, treasuries, regulators—Bitcoin diffused it through mathematics and electricity. Consensus emerged not from decree but from probability: the longest valid chain was the one that represented the most cumulative work. The network didn't decide who was honest; it made honesty cheaper than fraud.

Proof-of-work therefore reframed what finality meant. In traditional finance, settlement is legal and binary: a cheque clears, a transfer posts, a court enforces ownership. In Bitcoin, settlement is probabilistic. Each new block buried beneath layers of subsequent computation makes reversal exponentially harder, though never impossible. The deeper the chain, the stronger the confidence. This nuance—credibility through statistical improbability—was radical. Finality became not an absolute guarantee but a decaying probability of reversal, converging toward certainty as energy accumulated. It was trust quantified.

Two features made the system self-sustaining. First, the *difficulty adjustment* ensured that no single miner could dominate indefinitely. Every two weeks, the network recalibrated to maintain roughly ten-minute block intervals, regardless of total computing power. The algorithm adjusted its challenge like a central bank raising or lowering interest rates, but with no discretion or politics. Second, the *issuance schedule*—the halving of block rewards every 210,000 blocks—enforced monetary discipline by design. Where central banks expand money to manage crises, Bitcoin shrinks issuance as it matures. Together, difficulty and issuance formed an autonomous feedback loop: cost governs access; scarcity governs value; participation governs security.

This alignment of incentives was what Finney later called *the Nakamoto scheme*—a term he used admiringly, not cynically. The scheme worked because it made cheating economically irrational. To attack the network, one would need to control over half its computing power and sustain the expense of re-mining the chain while forfeiting legitimate rewards. The more valuable Bitcoin became, the more costly such an attack would be. Security scaled with price. Trust scaled with expenditure. The paradox—waste creates safety—offended many economists but proved resilient in practice. What looked inefficient in isolation was efficient in aggregate because it removed the need for bailouts, arbitration, or moral hazard.

This, then, was the bargain: neutrality at the price of throughput. Bitcoin could not process thousands of transactions per second, nor could it reverse mistakes or blacklist bad actors. What it offered instead was a form of digital settlement that treated every participant equally. One CPU, one vote; one block, one history. Speed was sacrificed for symmetry. The ten-minute rhythm became a kind of monetary heartbeat—steady, indifferent, incorruptible. The trade-off was philosophical as much as technical: Bitcoin optimised for fairness, not convenience.

The early years tested that commitment. In 2010, a user paid 10,000 bitcoins for two pizzas—a transaction that, by 2021 prices, would have exceeded $400 million. The anecdote became mythic, illustrating Bitcoin's transition from experiment to economy. By 2013, as price volatility and media attention grew, critics denounced proof-of-work as wasteful and slow. Yet the network continued to function exactly as designed. No central authority adjusted supply; no regulator paused withdrawals. Its neutrality was maddening precisely because it was credible. In a world accustomed to intervention, Bitcoin's silence during turmoil was disconcerting.

Still, the system's durability was not inevitable. Competing designs—most notably *proof-of-stake*—have since sought to replicate consensus without the energy cost. But these alternatives reveal what Bitcoin's design protects: a firewall between influence and control. In proof-of-stake systems, authority derives from ownership—those with more coins validate more blocks. In proof-of-work, authority derives from contribution—those who expend energy secure the network, regardless of holdings. The difference is moral as much as economic. One system privileges wealth; the other privileges effort. Nakamoto's bargain, in that light, was a wager on egalitarianism enforced by physics.

Yet the bargain is not without tension. As block rewards halve, miners must rely increasingly on transaction fees. This introduces a subtle feedback loop: if network usage drops, miners may switch off, weakening security; if fees rise too sharply, users may flee to cheaper alternatives. The design therefore assumes an equilibrium between demand and defence. It is an open question whether that equilibrium can persist as issuance approaches zero in the year 2140. The experiment is long-term by design; its full outcome will outlive its creator.

The motif that threads through this architecture is *cost as conscience.* Every block mined carries the weight of energy expended—a physical trace of human choice. Critics often reduce this to waste; proponents call it proof. The network's transparency transforms electricity into evidence. Like the minting of ancient coins, where each strike of metal bore the sovereign's stamp, Bitcoin's proof-of-work stamps each block with measurable sacrifice. In a digital era where value can be copied infinitely, Bitcoin's greatest innovation is to make duplication expensive again.

To see how this functions as governance, not gadgetry, consider the process of change. Every modification to the protocol—such as Segregated Witness (SegWit) in 2017 or Taproot in 2021—requires social consensus among miners, developers, and users. No one can compel an upgrade; participants must voluntarily adopt new rules. This decentralised procedure enforces what political theorist Friedrich Hayek once imagined but could not code: spontaneous order. Governance emerges from incentives, not from offices. The result is slow, messy, and remarkably stable. Where corporate networks patch bugs overnight, Bitcoin patches only when society agrees that it must. Its bureaucracy is measured in megawatts.

The bargain's counter-example lies in the systems it rejects. When central banks in 2020 launched unprecedented stimulus programmes, expanding balance sheets by trillions, their trust was political, not algorithmic. Their success depended on credibility—the belief that they *could* reverse expansion later. Bitcoin, by contrast, cannot promise discretion; it promises predictability. Its neutrality is structural. It cannot lie about its supply curve any more than gravity can lie about acceleration. The contrast is stark: one system requires perpetual reassurance; the other requires only computation.

Still, no rule is credible in a vacuum. Proof-of-work relies on human faith in the code's continuity, in miners' willingness to pay real-world costs for digital rewards, and in society's demand for non-sovereign value. The code itself is mute; belief animates it. The Nakamoto bargain therefore extends beyond economics—it is a social contract disguised as software. Participants accept energy expenditure, latency, and volatility in exchange for one intangible dividend: the right not to ask permission.

Twelve years after block 170, Hal Finney's wallet is silent, and Satoshi's identity remains unknown. But the ledger they helped ignite continues to advance, one block every ten minutes, recording a global conversation in numbers and proof. Each addition is an act of collective assertion: that neutrality can be engineered, that trust can be replaced by cost, and that rules can endure without rulers.

The unresolved question remains as elegant as it is unsettling: can a system that depends on waste for order, and on faith for neutrality, outlast the institutions it sought to transcend? The Nakamoto bargain holds for now—credibility traded for capacity, speed for sovereignty. But the price of incorruptibility, like the electricity that powers it, must be paid anew every ten minutes.

Forks, Ossification, and the Politics of Minimalism

On 23 May 2017 in New York, a group of exchanges, wallet firms, and mining companies gathered around a memorandum backed by Digital Currency Group. The "New York Agreement" proposed a bargain: activate Segregated Witness to improve transaction capacity, then hard fork later to raise the block size parameter. Signatures were collected at a hotel near Times Square. Cameras flashed; statements promised unity. By November, the hard fork half of the plan—SegWit2x—collapsed. The agreement unravelled not in courtrooms but in code repositories and node consoles, as thousands of operators refused to run the proposed changes. Weeks earlier, on 1

August, a separate faction had split off to create Bitcoin Cash. Two outcomes, one city, one year: a network that would change only when it could afford to, and a dissenting chain that would change when it wished. The message was unambiguous. The brake held.

The episode exposed Bitcoin's peculiar constitution. Change requires social coordination first, then code. Everyone must choose to upgrade; no one can be compelled. That asymmetry—the ease of refusal relative to the cost of imposition—creates guardrails that bias the system towards stasis. Minimalism is not an aesthetic; it is a policy. The effect is visible in behaviour rather than slogans: node operators decline binaries they distrust; miners signal support but cannot force it; exchanges hedge by listing both tickers when forks occur. The incentive landscape turns inertia into a defence. When in doubt, hold the line. It was a five-word rule, lived rather than announced.

Show, name, explain, implication. The 2017 block-size conflict shows the mechanism by which Bitcoin governs change. Name the actors: core developers publishing Bitcoin Improvement Proposals; large mining pools signalling intentions; companies backing agreements; independent node operators setting the final gate. Explain the process: proposals circulate on mailing lists; reference clients implement cautiously; miners signal readiness; users either adopt the new binaries or they do not. Implication: legitimacy in Bitcoin is not a harvest of signatures but an accretion of voluntary alignment. The brake—distributed refusal—outranks the accelerator.

The network's cultural minimalism rests on two technical choices that reduce conflict. First, soft forks that tighten rules are preferred over hard forks that loosen them. Soft forks let old nodes keep functioning, avoiding coercive upgrades. Second, feature scope is intentionally narrow. Bitcoin aspires to be a settlement layer: censorship-resistant, predictable, and slow to change. A narrow scope allows a thick consensus. We can observe the discipline in two moments. SegWit's activation in 2017 was engineered through paths that allowed dissenters to keep old software while the majority moved, culminating in a user-activated soft fork that asserted community agency. Taproot's activation in November 2021 used a time-bounded mechanism known as "Speedy Trial" that sought broad signalling before flipping the switch. Both upgrades were framed not as leaps forward but as adjustments that preserved the ledger's reliability. The visible behaviours were conservative: long lead times, extensive testing, and a bias toward backward compatibility. The implication is the chapter's thesis: upgrade conservatism functions as a security feature, not a failure of imagination.

Two further examples, concrete and checkable, clarify the politics at work. In July 2016, Ethereum executed a hard fork to reverse the DAO exploit, rewriting a portion of chain history to restore diverted funds. The move, debated openly and enacted decisively, led to the continued "Ethereum" and the minority "Ethereum Classic". The behaviour was visible: client teams shipped new versions; exchanges relabelled markets; miners chose sides. In contrast, Bitcoin during the same period refused to use a hard fork to solve capacity disputes, insisting on the safer path of a soft fork (SegWit) and off-chain scaling experiments. The implication is not that one community was right and the other wrong, but that different constitutional instincts were made legible. Ethereum valued expressive adaptability; Bitcoin valued ossified neutrality. Each paid a price it considered acceptable.

A second example sits within Bitcoin's own family of schisms. Bitcoin XT and Bitcoin Classic, earlier attempts (2015–2016) to change the block size through hard forks, achieved attention but failed to gain lasting traction. Their client downloads spiked, public endorsements accumulated, yet the share of full nodes running those implementations receded. The metric was simple: who actually upgraded? The decision was simpler: most did not. The implication is stark. In Bitcoin, the median node operator has an effective veto. Nothing compels adoption beyond persuasion and proof.

The credible counter-example is that ossification can foreclose necessary evolution. Critics argue that minimalism risks calcifying suboptimal design, leaving the base layer too rigid to adapt to new threats or to incorporate evident improvements. They point to long deliberations around signature schemes, fee estimation, and mempool policies as evidence that slowness can hinder responsiveness. The reconciliation is sober. A settlement layer that aspires to be a neutral base for the next century must prefer unattractive survival to elegant change. The costs of slowness are real; the costs of hasty centralisation are greater. The brake cannot be discarded simply because the road ahead looks straight.

The motif that will recur is the *keel*. A ship's keel adds weight and drag; it also keeps the vessel upright in heavy weather. Bitcoin's keel is its politics of minimalism. It drags on speed; it stabilises direction. You see the keel every time an enticing feature is deferred, every time a draft BIP is withdrawn for lack of consensus, every time a loud faction finds itself unable to compel the quiet majority. The network prefers boredom to brilliance when brilliance threatens coordination. That is not romance. It is risk management.

Minimalism is not passivity. It is an allocation of where complexity belongs. Bitcoin's bias is to keep the base layer primitive and push experimentation to edges: second layers, client tooling, and market infrastructure. This separation of powers reduces correlated failure. If a lightning channel fails, the base chain is there as court of final appeal; if a wallet misprices fees, the settlement rules remain untouched. The behaviour is everywhere in the ecosystem: companies innovate without begging protocol custodians; researchers test new ideas on testnets; the chain itself barely notices. The implication is strategic: a quiet base invites a loud frontier.

The politics of minimalism also rests on who bears costs when changes go wrong. In centralised systems, a mistake can be reversed by executive decree. In decentralised systems, a misstep may be irrevocable. That asymmetry increases the required confidence for any change. It is why the cultural bar for activation is so high, and why soft forks are the default: it lowers the worst-case harm to dissenters. The behavioural metric is revealing: operators ask "Can I safely do nothing?" If the answer is yes, legitimacy grows. If the answer is no, fragility grows. The constant preference for options that respect non-participation reflects a constitutional ethic, not merely a technical one.

There is a further reason why ossification is a feature: it deters capture. The slower the base layer moves, the harder it is for concentrated interests—states, corporations, cartels—to bend it to their will through regulation or procurement. A protocol that promises to change on request invites lobbying. A protocol that barely changes forces intermediaries to adapt around it. The behavioural evidence lies in the failure of well-funded efforts to dictate outcomes in 2017, and in the relative futility of signalling campaigns that lack grassroots node consent. The implication is subtle but profound: slowness is a moat.

Yet minimalism requires maintenance. A keel rots if ignored. Client diversity matters; so does the distribution of nodes across jurisdictions; so does the proportion of mining power in any one region or pool. Upgrade conservatism does not absolve the community from tending to these practicalities. It demands it. The behaviours to watch are tractable: which implementations dominate production nodes; how many independent teams can ship consensus-critical code; how resistant the network is to legal pressure applied to exchanges and miners. Minimalism does not mean indifference. It means stewardship expressed as refusal.

The politics of forks reveals the same pattern through a sharper lens. A fork is a pressure valve. It allows disagreement to exit without bloodshed. It also imposes costs: network effects fragment; ticker symbols dilute; the uninitiated are confused. Each fork therefore tests the community's appetite for purity versus coherence. Bitcoin Cash in 2017 chose throughput over alignment with minimalism; its subsequent proliferation into further variants illustrated how hard it is to stop once you start using forking to settle ordinary policy disputes. The main chain's inertia looks less like timidity when viewed against that entropy.

Ossification is often caricatured as a terminal state. It is better described as a direction of travel. Each successful soft fork, carefully scoped and widely adopted, can add expressive capacity without abandoning the ethic of restraint. Taproot's enhancements to privacy and scripting are a case in point: more potential at the margins, no change to the monetary core. This is the pattern to expect if minimalism endures—rare, well-justified changes that preserve predictability while pruning attack surface. The brake is pressed; the ship still moves.

What, finally, does all this say about neutrality? A settlement layer that refuses to hurry is harder to bully. A protocol that refuses ornate features is harder to corrupt. The cost is clear: users must build complexity above and around the base, accepting a layered architecture where immediacy and expressivity live off-chain or in side systems. The reward is equally clear: a base that can credibly serve as court of last resort because it is not continuously renovating itself.

The unresolved question remains the honest one. How much ossification is enough? At what point does the brake prevent necessary evasive action—against new cryptographic threats, unexpected fee dynamics, or geopolitical shocks—and at what point does releasing it invite exactly the capture minimalism was meant to resist? The keel steadies the ship. But seas change. Who decides when to add more wood, and who pays if the hull, once altered, no longer runs true?

Security Budgets and the End of Subsidies

On 20 April 2024, at block 840,000, Bitcoin's block subsidy fell from 6.25 to 3.125 BTC. No committee voted. No central bank briefed markets. The code's schedule advanced by exactly one block, and the flow of new coins halved. Miners who had invested in hardware and power saw their primary revenue line cut in two, instantly and everywhere. Some switched off less efficient machines within hours. Others chased lower electricity prices. All of them checked the mempool and recalibrated bids for hash power. A simple arithmetic truth asserted itself—if fees did not rise, security would fall. The bill must be paid.

Show this pressure; name the mechanism; explain the trade; map the stakes. Bitcoin's security budget is the sum of block subsidies and transaction fees received by miners. The first term decays by design; the second must grow or at least persist if the network's credible neutrality is to remain funded. Fees are not an optional tip. They are the price users collectively pay to keep the guards at the gate. If demand for settlement is thin, guards go hungry. If guards go hungry, adversaries take notice. Every halving therefore converts an abstract long-run question into a concrete near-run test: will fee markets mature fast enough to finance incorruptibility as subsidies diminish?

Two recent, verifiable episodes illustrate how demand translates into defence. In May 2023, inscriptions and BRC-20 minting congested Bitcoin's mempool for days; multiple blocks paid miners more in fees than in subsidy, a reversal of the decade-long norm. The behaviour was obvious to anyone watching: sat/vByte bids climbed, low-fee transactions lingered, and mining pools adjusted templates to capture high-fee packages. Whatever one thinks of the novelty that drove it, that burst of usage demonstrated a principle: sustained, varied demand can fund security without touching issuance. A second episode came with the April 2024 halving itself. In the hours around block 840,000, ceremonial and speculative demand briefly pushed fees to levels that again eclipsed the new 3.125 BTC subsidy on several blocks. Then they subsided. The implication is sobering. Spikes are not a business model. A settlement layer needs a durable base of transactions that are willing to pay for finality week after week, not just during fads or rites of passage.

The motif that threads this subchapter is plain: *who pays the guards?* Every claim about "hardness", "neutrality", or "finality" eventually reduces to that question. In a proof-of-work system, the answer is visible in miner income statements block by block. Fee share matters. Fee persistence matters. Fee diversity matters. If those indicators weaken as subsidies fade, the security budget shrinks, and the cost to attack falls relative to the reward of doing so. Credible neutrality becomes less credible.

Why does the budget matter? Because adversaries measure, too. An attacker weighing a deep reorganisation, a censorship campaign, or sustained hash-rate rental compares their expected cost to the potential gain—whether that gain is double-spending a large settlement, wrecking market confidence, or achieving political ends. If miner revenue collapses, honest hash retreats, and the same absolute spend buys more relative influence. That is not a prophecy; it is arithmetic. Neutrality is not a state of grace; it is a funded service.

To make these dynamics concrete, move through the claims with the discipline of Show → Name → Explain → Implication. Show: in fee-rich periods, exchanges lower the number of confirmations they demand for large withdrawals; in fee-poor periods, they often raise it. Name: these are risk management policies posted by major venues and adjusted with mempool conditions. Explain: deeper confirmation requirements price in the possibility of reorgs when the honest chain's cost of defence is low; shallower requirements reflect confidence that reorgs would be prohibitively expensive. Implication: market actors already treat the security budget as a variable, not a constant. Neutrality is probabilistic in code and priced in practice.

Two further, named examples sharpen the frame. First, Ethereum Classic suffered multiple 51% attacks in August 2020 when adversaries rented hash power to re-mine history; exchanges responded by raising confirmation counts into the thousands and, at times, pausing deposits entirely. Although not Bitcoin, the case demonstrates how thin security budgets invite opportunistic assault and how markets react by degrading user experience to maintain safety. Second, Bitcoin Gold was attacked in 2018 and again in 2020 via similar hash-rental strategies. The visible behaviours—longer confirmation windows, delistings, and forensic reports by exchanges and analytics firms—were reminders that proof-of-work's neutrality is funded neutrality, and that budget shortfalls get exploited. The implication is blunt: if you do not pay guards enough, someone pays to push past them.

A credible counter-argument insists that Bitcoin is different: its scale deters attack, its brand attracts users, and its hardware footprint cannot be trivially rented. There is force in this. Bitcoin's mining ecosystem is deeper, its liquidity broader, and its chain analytics far more watched than smaller networks. The reconciliation, however, returns to first principles. Advantages of scale and scrutiny are helpful but not substitutes for revenue. They raise the baseline cost of attack; they do not eliminate it. If fee income dwindled for months, incentives would shift at the margin in ways an attacker could model. A settlement layer should not rely on aura when it can rely on invoices.

This is where the politics of minimalism intersects the economics of security. By keeping the base layer's feature set narrow and change slow, Bitcoin aims to serve as a high-integrity court of final appeal. But courts must be funded. In sovereign systems, taxes pay judges. In Bitcoin, fees pay miners. The question becomes operational: what does a healthy fee market look like for a conservative settlement base? The checklist is empirical, not devotional.

First, *fee share over time*: measure the proportion of miner revenue coming from fees across rolling windows—weekly, monthly, yearly. Healthy security budgets show fee shares that rise after each halving and stabilise above a floor, not just spike episodically. Second, *demand diversity*: observe the composition of transactions. Are fees supported by several independent sources—exchange batched withdrawals, layer-two channel opens and closes, cross-border treasury movements, timestamping commitments, and periodic consolidation—not just by a single fad? Monocultures are brittle. Third, *mempool persistence*: track how often, and for how long, the mempool remains non-empty at fee levels that price rationally for next-block inclusion. A perpetually empty mempool is a red flag; a perpetually jammed one signals other problems. Fourth, *latency tolerance*: watch user behaviour. Do institutional users and payment processors commit to wait longer and pay more during congestion, or do they flee to custodial rails? Patience is a revealed preference. Fifth, *fee elasticity*: when demand surges, do fees climb smoothly or snap? Smooth curves suggest depth; snaps suggest shallowness. Sixth, *pool behaviour*: monitor whether pools include low-fee transactions that carry non-monetary value to them (e.g., client relationships), or relentlessly optimise only for fee per weight. The former may signal cross-subsidy; the latter shows hard reliance on the market. Seventh, *orphan and reorg rates*: elevated rates in fee-poor regimes may hint at miners gambling on short-term tactics like fee sniping rather than building the longest chain. That is a canary.

Thread the motif again. Who pays the guards, and how regularly? The answer should be: many users, for many reasons, most of the time. When that is true, the guards carry on, indifferent to fads. When it is not, neutrality leans on hope.

A common objection asserts that second-layer protocols will shoulder most transactional demand, starving the base of fees. The fear is coherent but incomplete. If second-layer channels open, rebalance, and close on-chain; if rollups and sidechains post periodic commitments or fraud proofs; if custodians batch large settlements rather than stream small withdrawals—then the base layer may process fewer individual payments but more *expensive* state transitions. That is a good profile for a court. The metric to watch is not raw transaction count but *value-weighted demand for finality*. If the median on-chain event becomes heavier—closing a channel with a year's worth of flow rather than buying coffee—the fee market can remain deep on lower volume. The settlement court hears fewer cases, each of higher value, and charges accordingly.

Miners, for their part, adapt. After the 2024 halving, public mining firms reported sharpened focus on power contracts, firmware efficiency, and curtailment deals with grid operators. These behaviours matter to security budgets because they change miners' break-even thresholds and their willingness to mine during fee droughts. Lower costs widen the range of fee conditions under which honest hash remains profitable. Here, too, markets already measure. Analysts track hash price (revenue per unit of hash), the distribution of machine vintages in the active fleet, and regional power mix. While these are business metrics, they map back to neutrality by indicating how robustly the network can maintain work when fees sag.

There is also the adversary's ledger to consider. Suppose a state actor contemplates censoring transactions for geo-political reasons rather than profit. Their calculus differs: they may accept sustained losses to achieve policy goals. The defence in such a case is not only price but pluralism—geographical dispersion of miners; diversity of pool operators; personal custody of nodes; and the cultural expectation that clients will default to versions that resist blacklists. Yet even here, the fee market matters. If honest miners earn enough to withstand targeted pressure, if defectors are quickly replaced by entrants lured by margins, if pools that censor lose share because non-censoring pools earn more, then politics meets economics and retreats. Funding constrains zeal.

One must also face the nightmare scenario: chronic fee poverty. Imagine months of low utilisation, thin fee income, and consolidating mining ownership. The temptation to chase short-term revenue through strategies like fee sniping or out-of-band payments grows. A miner may withhold a block to capture a large fee in the next, or accept private transaction bundles that do not transparently compete in the public mempool. The behaviour has already been documented in other ecosystems. Its appearance at scale on Bitcoin would downgrade neutrality, because inclusion would no longer be an open auction but a patchwork of side deals. The remedy is the same: a richer public fee market that outbids private arrangements.

The counter-example to fee pessimism is historical. Across three previous halvings—2012, 2016, 2020—hash power fell temporarily, then resumed climbing as price and participation adjusted. Security budgets recovered, helped by cycles of interest and the onboarding of institutions. The limitation is clear: past cycles occurred under higher subsidies and different competitive landscapes. Replaying them forward demands caution. The reconciliation is to treat history as scenario, not guarantee. The checklist exists precisely to replace nostalgia with measurement.

Circle back to the motif once more. The base layer is a courthouse with no tax base. It lives on filing fees. The clerk does not care why you filed—remittance, channel closure, treasury move, art, audit—but the clerk must be paid. A courthouse that cannot pay clerks does not slowly degrade. It abruptly fails.

So the forward test stands. After each halving, does the ratio of fees to subsidy rise and stay risen? Do more independent users choose to anchor to the base, even as second layers flourish? Do miners earn enough from the auction most of the time to keep their machines honourably pointed, even when prices dip? If not, which dial will society move—accept higher latency and fees to thicken the market, innovate in fee aggregation to widen payer bases, or revisit base-layer rules at the risk of loosening the constitutional brake?

Neutrality is a budget line. Who pays the guards, and for how long?

What Bitcoin Optimises For—and What It Sacrifices

On 16 March 2013 in Nicosia, queues snaked outside cash machines as Cyprus's banks shut their doors. The Eurogroup had endorsed a rescue that would impose losses on large depositors; withdrawals were capped; transfers abroad were restricted. ATMs spat out rationed notes. Phones buzzed with new limits and new rules. The gate had closed. Two weeks later, on 25 March, Bank of Cyprus depositors learned that a bail-in would crystallise losses on balances above €100,000. The architecture of finance had chosen survival over liquidity. That day, comparisons with "digital cash" were not about speed or fees. They were about control. Who can lock a vault? Who can't?

Bitcoin was built to answer that question with an unyielding design. It prioritises two properties above all else: censorship resistance and predictable issuance. It refuses expressive code at the base layer. It declines speed. It treats finality as a probability that hardens with work, not with signatures on a policy memo. This is not a deficit of ambition; it is a deliberate trade. The motif that will recur here is stark: *the locked gate and the open wire*. Fintech prides itself on smoother gates; Bitcoin insists on keeping the wire open.

Start from first principles and proceed by evidence. Show, name, explain, implication.

Show: in March 2013, the Cypriot state, the European Central Bank, and the International Monetary Fund enforced capital controls to prevent a banking collapse. Name: the Eurogroup communiqué and Bank of Cyprus bail-in terms were public, and the controls were executed by banks subject to law. Explain: when states defend their fiscal core, they prioritise elasticity over private claims; bank deposits are liabilities in a hierarchy that bends under stress. Implication: any payment system integrated with that hierarchy inherits the capacity to freeze and ration. The locked gate is not a bug. It is a power.

Bitcoin's base layer is engineered to resist that power. Nodes do not know passports. Miners assemble transactions by fee, not by identity.

There is no switch to reverse history or ring-fence address ranges by decree. The visible behaviours follow: a valid transaction that pays sufficient fees is relayed, included, and then buried under further proof-of-work; reversing it costs more energy than most attackers can sustainably burn. The protocol's schedule—issuance halves roughly every four years—removes discretion at the monetary core. These are not slogans. They are design commitments that show up as code paths and confirmation rules.

Minimal expressivity is the price of those commitments. Scripts are intentionally constrained. There is no Turing-complete virtual machine at the base. Contractual richness lives at the edges—multisignature policies, timelocks, and layered constructions—rather than in a general-purpose state machine. The implication is practical: if you compare Bitcoin to a retail payments processor or a smart-contract platform, you will find it slow, spartan, and unaccommodating. That is the category error. Bitcoin is a settlement base that optimises for *who cannot be stopped*, not a checkout widget that optimises for *who can be on-boarded quickly*.

Case studies reveal the contrast. In October 2020, as Nigerian protesters rallied under the #EndSARS banner, local payment processors cut off donation flows after regulatory pressure. The Feminist Coalition, a prominent fundraising group, posted a Bitcoin address and continued receiving support. Name the behaviour: banks complied with directives; the blockchain ignored them. Explain: bank transfers ride rails that route through centralised chokepoints; Bitcoin's relay network routes by policy embedded in software. Implication: censorship resistance is not a promise; it is a refusal to possess the lever that would make censorship easy.

A second case, Canada in February 2022, shows how blacklists operate in mature democracies under stress. The federal government invoked the Emergencies Act during the convoy protests and directed financial institutions to freeze specific accounts. Some cryptocurrency addresses were circulated in public as assets of concern. Exchanges with custody complied; self-custodied funds remained controllable only by holders of the keys. The behaviour split cleanly along custody lines. The implication is not that Bitcoin nullifies law; it is that Bitcoin changes who must be persuaded. If an exchange holds your coins, policy can reach them. If you hold your keys, policy must reach *you.*

Now the sacrifice. By pushing discretion out of the base layer, Bitcoin accepts throughput limits and latency. Blocks target ten minutes. Fees rise during congestion. Chargebacks do not exist. Error recovery is hard. A bank can reverse a mis-sent wire if the counterparty agrees; a miner cannot be asked—much less forced—to resurrect a spent input. The behavioural consequences are familiar to serious users: wait for confirmations; batch transactions; price fees with care; build second layers for immediacy. The open wire keeps running; it does not bend for convenience.

A further sacrifice is expressivity. When developers on expressive chains can deploy complex contracts to automate markets or encode conditional logic, Bitcoin insists on keeping complex behaviour at the margins. Lightning channels negotiate off-chain; covenants and more advanced primitives are added cautiously, if at all. This conservatism is not a lack of imagination; it is defence of the base. Every new opcode would be an attack surface and a vector for social pressure to "patch quickly" during failures. Minimalism, as argued earlier, is a keel. It slows you down; it keeps you upright.

Tether two more named, checkable examples to the frame and watch the motif hold. First, sanctions. The U.S. Treasury's Office of Foreign Assets Control has listed specific Bitcoin addresses associated with ransomware actors in multiple advisories since 2018. Custodial platforms geofence and monitor those addresses; regulated businesses harden controls. Yet the base layer does not "block" them. The ledger records what is valid by rules indifferent to identity; enforcement lives at the edges—in exchanges, banks, and mixers—where law reaches people. The locked gate is moved to a doorway that can see faces; the open wire remains blind. The implication: Bitcoin's neutrality is structural, but users live in jurisdictions. The protocol refuses to be a policeman; the polity will do that job wherever it can.

Second, capital controls beyond crisis. Argentina has imposed varying limits on foreign currency purchases and transfers for years, often tightening rules during inflation spikes. People respond with behaviour, not theory: they seek dollar substitutes, route payments through informal channels, and experiment with digital assets. Where exchanges are forced to KYC and report, Bitcoin settles to self-custody or peer-to-peer trades. Every tightening of the formal gate pushes more value across the open wire. The implication is twofold. Bitcoin's purpose becomes visible where the gate keeps closing. Its sacrifices become visible where fintech shines—refund flows, consumer protections, instant card reversals. Different aims, different tools.

A credible counter-example is worth facing head-on: high-compliance, high-throughput payment networks can and do serve billions with reliability and recourse. Card networks clear millions of transactions per minute; real-time payment rails post within seconds; fraud departments monitor patterns and reimburse victims. Measure the behaviours: chargeback windows; dispute resolution rates; settlement times measured in seconds; consumer satisfaction metrics. By those measures, Bitcoin fares poorly. The reconciliation is conceptual, not rhetorical. These networks optimise for a different mandate—*service with permissioned reversibility*—and they succeed within it. The category error occurs when they are presented as substitutes for a permissionless, non-reversible settlement base. A courtroom is not a cash register. Judge them by their charters.

Predictable issuance is the second pillar of Bitcoin's optimisation and an equally sharp trade. The schedule is fixed at inception; halving events reduce the block subsidy on a known cadence until it approaches zero. This constraint has two consequences. First, it removes the temptation to inflate supply for expediency. Second, it forbids the use of discretionary monetary tools to smooth shocks. A central bank can cut rates, expand reserves, or buy assets to backstop markets. Bitcoin can do none of those things. The behaviour shows. During market panics, central banks host press conferences; in Bitcoin, the mempool simply thickens and clears. The implication is austere: stability is purchased ex ante through rules, not ex post through interventions. Users absorb volatility; the system refuses to.

The motif returns: the locked gate and the open wire. Under strain, states tighten gates because they can. Under strain, Bitcoin keeps the wire open because it must. The distinction is not moral; it is constitutional. One design manages society by discretion and promises to use it well; the other manages itself by refusal and promises to keep refusing. Each is vulnerable where the other is strong. A society that relies only on locked gates risks overreach and exclusion. A network that relies only on an open wire risks rough edges and hard landings.

This framing clarifies debates about blacklists. Calls emerge periodically for protocol-level filters to exclude "bad" addresses. Such proposals misunderstand the architecture. The base layer does not know who is bad; it knows only who is valid under consensus rules. Embedding identity into validity would collapse neutrality into adjudication. The costs would be immediate: miners would face jurisdictional fights over which list to adopt; nodes would fork over definitions; fees would encode politics. The open wire would become a gated community. The sacrifice would be the point.

That does not absolve Bitcoin of trade-off pain. When fees surge, poorer users are priced out of base-layer settlement. When latency rises, time-sensitive commerce hesitates. The response has been architectural: build layers that inherit base-layer guarantees while offering speed and lower cost—Lightning for bilateral payments; sidechains and roll-up-like constructions for batched settlement; collaborative custody for resilience. Each adds complexity. Each accepts new risks. Each preserves the base layer's refusal to confiscate or to inflate. The direction of travel is consistent: keep the open wire narrow and strong; let the bridges carry traffic above it.

What of corporate comparisons—"TPS", "latency", "cost per transaction"—that frame Bitcoin as obsolete? Replace abstractions with decisions. A retailer cares whether a charge can be reversed when a stolen card is used; a protest movement cares whether a donation can be frozen at the bank; a treasurer cares whether cross-border transfers will clear under sanctions. Different contexts, different metrics. The right comparison is not Bitcoin versus cards. It is Bitcoin's settlement assurances versus those of any system that can be stopped by a phone call. Measure who must be persuaded. Measure how many gates stand between payer and payee. Count them.

There is a final sacrifice that deserves emphasis: forgiveness. Systems designed for consumer finance build processes to unwind mistakes—chargebacks, arbitration, customer support. Bitcoin has no central help desk. A mis-typed address is a permanent loss; an under-funded fee during congestion may strand a transaction. The behaviour this induces is responsible if inconvenient: test sends, QR codes, hardware wallets with checks, multi-party policies, and education. The implication is cultural. Bitcoin pushes competence to the edge. Some will find that empowering; others will find it exclusionary until tooling makes competence easier.

The open question, and it should remain open, is how far the prioritisation should go. How much throughput can be conceded to preserve censorship resistance, and how much expressivity can be admitted without inviting capture? How often should the base layer change to accommodate new threats, and how quickly should layers above it evolve to widen access for those priced out during fee spikes? The gate will keep closing in some places. The wire will keep attracting those who need it. The test is whether a society can accept that both designs must coexist—and whether it knows which one to reach for when the gate slams shut.

Chapter 3
State Without State: Ethereum and the Programmable Ledger

On 17 June 2016, an autonomous piece of software began draining millions of dollars' worth of ether from a crowd-funded investment vehicle called The DAO. There were no masked intruders, no servers seized. The code simply did what it was written to do: exploit a recursive call flaw to divert funds. The contract was law, until the community decided otherwise. Weeks later, on 20 July, the Ethereum network executed a hard fork to reverse the exploit. One chain accepted the rewrite; another refused. The split gave the world two names—Ethereum and Ethereum Classic—and a lasting parable: when machines rule the money, governance never disappears, it only moves.

That summer crystallised Ethereum's grand experiment: to build a *state without a state*—a programmable ledger that could host not only payments but entire institutions in code. Bitcoin had demonstrated that money could move without banks. Ethereum wanted to show that agreements could execute without intermediaries. Its founding promise, unveiled by Vitalik Buterin in 2015, was radical in both scope and subtlety: not merely to store value but to compute it. If Bitcoin was digital gold, Ethereum was a digital polity—mutable, expressive, and always negotiating the limits of its own power.

This chapter begins in that tension. Ethereum replaces the singular function of a monetary network with a general-purpose computer—a shared state machine that anyone can write to but no one can own. It is money that thinks, or rather, code that counts. The promise is seductive: *if we can trust the execution, we can disintermediate the institution.* A token can represent a share, a vote, a deed, a piece of art, or an automated market. Yet the cost of this expressivity is complexity, and complexity breeds both power and fragility. The more one can build, the more one can break. Each contract multiplies the number of dependencies; each dependency expands the surface for failure. The DAO hack was not an anomaly—it was the first constitutional crisis of a programmable state.

From this core paradox arises the political economy of *blockspace*. Every computation consumes gas, and gas costs money. Ethereum's ledger is not infinite; it is a market, and like all markets, it reveals hierarchies of access and advantage. Validators set priorities; users bid for inclusion; searchers extract value from order flow. Blockspace becomes a rationed commons where efficiency collides with fairness. The jargon—MEV, base fee, tip—is the language of a political system learning to price its own bandwidth. What was once "free execution" becomes an economy of congestion and strategy. Each transaction is a vote with money on what matters most.

Yet Ethereum's ambition extends beyond economics. Its periodic upgrades—Metropolis, Constantinople, London, Merge, Shanghai—are less like software patches and more like constitutional amendments. They redefine rights, redistribute power, and rewrite incentives. Each upgrade must achieve a form of social legitimacy before it becomes technical reality. Consensus is not only a computational goal but a cultural one. The Merge in September 2022, which shifted the network from proof-of-work to proof-of-stake, required years of deliberation and coordination across thousands of independent actors. The success of that migration demonstrated that Ethereum's governance, while decentralised, could still act with purpose. Yet it also underscored the central paradox of a "state without state": the code may execute automatically, but legitimacy is earned socially.

Ethereum's modularity—its much-lauded *composability*—compounds both its beauty and its brittleness. DeFi builders liken it to Lego: protocols snap together to create emergent functionality. Uniswap provides liquidity; Aave lends; Maker mints stablecoins; Curve arbitrages stability; all link through tokens and contracts. But the metaphor conceals a systemic truth: when one brick cracks, the tower shudders. Smart contracts share dependencies; stablecoins rely on price feeds; lending protocols depend on liquidity pools; liquidity pools depend on stablecoins. Correlation hides in code. The failure of one link can cascade across dozens. The DeFi summer of 2020 proved that decentralisation does not mean decoupling. Each composable innovation adds both utility and contagion.

The motif that threads through this chapter is one of mirrors and margins. Ethereum reflects our urge to formalise trust in code—to build machines that arbitrate where humans once debated. Yet, like all mirrors, it distorts. For every instance where smart contracts remove friction, they introduce opacity. For every layer of automation, there arises a new human question: who wrote the rules, who audits them, and who bears the loss when automation misfires? The DAO fork, the Merge, and the recurring debates over gas fees and MEV distribution are not just episodes of protocol politics—they are chapters in the constitutional history of a digital society still writing its charter.

Ethereum's significance reaches far beyond the speculative heat of its markets. It offers a test case for how programmable systems can hold value, execute law, and evolve without sovereign permission. Whether it succeeds or fragments will shape how future systems balance code and consent, automation and accountability. In a decade defined by algorithmic governance and AI-mediated decisions, Ethereum's ongoing experiment asks a question that matters well beyond finance: *Can we design trust without a state—and survive our own success?*

The pages that follow trace this question through four dimensions: the shift from money to machines; the economics of gas and blockspace; the politics of upgrades as constitutional moments; and the fragile symphony of composability that defines decentralised finance. Each section dissects not only the technology but the governance logic it encodes—the implicit constitutions written into software and markets alike.

Ethereum is not merely a blockchain. It is a rehearsal for digital self-government, complete with its own taxation (gas), judiciary (consensus), legislature (governance forums), and dissent (forks). To study it is to study how power behaves when it loses its buildings and its badges, but keeps its logic. That is the state without state—a republic of code, forever balancing autonomy against fragility, and still discovering what it truly governs.

From Money to Machines

On 30 July 2015, a new kind of machine came online. The Ethereum network launched its *Frontier* release, enabling users not only to send tokens but to upload software to a shared ledger—programs that could hold, transfer, and even destroy value without human intermediaries. Within a day, the first smart contracts began to appear: simple lotteries, escrow systems, and token prototypes written in Solidity, a language that looked like a bridge between law and code. In those early blocks, the line between finance and computation began to dissolve. What had started as a decentralised currency experiment now promised an entire economy of autonomous logic. The monetary ledger had become a programmable world computer.

The leap was conceptual as much as technical. Bitcoin had proven that digital money could exist without a central bank. Ethereum proposed that *rules themselves* could run without a ruler. A Turing-complete virtual machine—capable of executing any computable instruction—would host contracts, organisations, and assets as lines of code secured by consensus. A transaction was no longer merely a transfer; it was a trigger. The motif that threads through this subchapter is the *machine that obeys no master*. Each advance in expressive power widened its potential and multiplied its risks. Every new form of autonomy created a new vector of fragility.

Show → Name → Explain → Implication. The pattern begins with The DAO. In April 2016, an ambitious experiment by the German start-up Slock.it launched what it called a "decentralised autonomous organisation"—a self-governing investment fund run entirely on Ethereum. Investors sent 12 million ether, worth about US$150 million at the time, into a contract with rules embedded in code. There was no board, no legal entity, only logic. When a vulnerability was exploited in June 2016, draining about one-third of the funds, the system behaved exactly as written, not as intended. The exploit was not a hack in the conventional sense; it was a mirror showing what absolute automation looks like when the code contains a flaw. The fork that followed—splitting Ethereum into two chains—marked the first constitutional crisis of programmable finance. The implication endures: automation removes discretion until discretion is needed most.

Ethereum's architecture—its *world state*—is a single, evolving ledger shared by all nodes. Every smart contract and every token operates on this same canvas. This composability enables near-instant innovation. Developers build lending protocols that call price oracles, stablecoins that draw liquidity from automated exchanges, and governance systems that coordinate upgrades across thousands of participants. Yet the same composability couples risk. In March 2020, during the Covid-19 market crash, MakerDAO's collateral auctions failed to clear properly as Ethereum's gas prices spiked. A handful of arbitrageurs exploited network congestion to acquire millions of dollars' worth of collateral for almost nothing. Show the behaviour: bots submitting zero-bid transactions; miners selecting the highest-fee orders; validators following economic incentives, not ethical instincts. Name it: the "Black Thursday" incident. Explain: under extreme conditions, the coordination machinery jammed. Implication: when every function is code, every crisis is computational.

The idea of *Turing-complete finance*—a ledger that can perform any logical operation—reshapes the meaning of "financial product". Traditional instruments are static contracts enforced by courts; Ethereum contracts are dynamic agents enforced by consensus. This allows for decentralised exchanges such as Uniswap, where pools of liquidity price assets through automated formulas rather than human market-makers. It enables lending platforms like Aave, where collateralisation and liquidation rules execute automatically. These systems replace institutional procedures with deterministic processes, trading legal certainty for algorithmic precision. Yet precision can be brittle. When oracles misreport, algorithms obey regardless. The open wire does not reason; it computes.

To see this duality in practice, consider two cases where expressive code produced both power and peril. In 2020, Compound Finance popularised "yield farming", distributing governance tokens to users who provided liquidity. Within months, similar systems proliferated. The behaviour was measurable: billions of dollars in value locked in smart contracts, with transaction fees rising in tandem. This composability ignited what became known as *DeFi summer*—a frenzy of permissionless innovation. Yet by 2022, several high-profile exploits, including the $130 million hack of Cream Finance and the $600 million Poly Network breach, exposed how interdependence amplified risk. A bug in one component cascaded through protocols that had reused its logic. The power to build anything had become the power to misbuild everything.

The credible counter-example comes from Ethereum's Layer 2 and auditing ecosystems. Rather than abandoning complexity, they attempt to contain it. Formal verification tools, multi-signature governance, and staged upgrade processes represent attempts to import the prudence of institutional design into a permissionless system. Rollups like Arbitrum and Optimism experiment with constrained execution environments to balance flexibility with safety. The reconciliation lies in a paradox: the very transparency that makes Ethereum auditable also makes it exploitable. Every contract is public; every vulnerability is visible. Security must therefore evolve as an ongoing negotiation between openness and defence. In this sense, Ethereum behaves less like a company than like a *constitution in flux*—a living arrangement whose norms and protections are perpetually rewritten in code.

The visible behaviour of developers reflects this political economy. Each contract deployment is a commitment of real capital; each bug bounty is a form of delegated trust. Teams announce audits by firms such as Trail of Bits or OpenZeppelin not as compliance but as signals of legitimacy. Security culture becomes reputation. A well-written white paper is no longer sufficient; the social layer must believe that the code's logic is fair. When that belief fails, capital flees. The *machine that obeys no master* still depends on collective faith that its builders have behaved honourably.

Ethereum's virtual machine turns financial relationships into computational dependencies. The economic cost of computation—the gas fee—translates abstract logic into measurable scarcity. Gas prices surge during network congestion, rationing blockspace as if it were urban land. Here, the behaviour of users reveals an invisible hierarchy: arbitrage bots outbid retail traders; complex contracts crowd out simple transfers; activity concentrates where fees justify themselves. In effect, Turing-complete finance recreates political economy in miniature. Every transaction is a micro-vote on what blockspace is worth, and every validator tallies those votes according to incentive, not sympathy. This reality exposes a deeper truth: decentralisation distributes power but does not dissolve it; it converts political authority into economic priority.

Power and fragility rise together because the system's guarantees depend on its participation. A contract's logic is worthless if no validator executes it honestly, just as an exchange rate peg fails when no one defends it. Ethereum's consensus provides the mechanical layer of trust, but the surrounding institutions—auditors, oracles, user communities—provide the interpretive layer. In that sense, Ethereum is not post-institutional; it is *meta-institutional.* It transforms old hierarchies into interlocking protocols whose legitimacy depends on continuous coordination. The cost of coordination is visible every time the network upgrades, debates fee models, or responds to an exploit. Every constitutional moment tests whether decentralised order can endure its own flexibility.

The motif returns: the machine that obeys no master, but whose survival still requires care. Turing-completeness allows the creation of autonomous agents—DAOs that vote, treasuries that allocate, stablecoins that regulate supply. Yet autonomy is not immunity. When Terra's algorithmic stablecoin UST collapsed in May 2022, erasing tens of billions in market value, the code did not fail alone. Its assumptions about demand, arbitrage, and collateral all derived from human confidence. As that confidence vanished, the machine kept executing, dutifully printing itself into oblivion. The event was not merely a financial loss; it was a philosophical one. It showed that even in fully automated systems, the boundary between machine logic and social belief is porous.

A quiet lesson emerges from these histories. Ethereum's genius lies in its ambition to generalise Bitcoin's narrow promise: from sound money to sound computation. But its fragility lies in the same move. As the ledger expands to host everything from games to governance, the scope of what can break expands exponentially. Each improvement—faster execution, richer languages, more expressive contracts—tightens the feedback loop between creativity and catastrophe. The engine of innovation is also the amplifier of failure.

The forward test, then, is diagnostic. How much autonomy can a society entrust to machines that execute exactly as written but never as judged? How should developers and users weigh the speed of iteration against the gravity of consensus? Ethereum's evolution from money to machines invites both exhilaration and caution. The next failure will not come from ignorance but from success—because the more capable the system becomes, the more it will demand that we define what *obedience without discretion* should mean when billions depend on it.

Gas, Fees, and the Political Economy of Blockspace

On 5 August 2021, the Ethereum network activated the London upgrade, introducing EIP-1559. Overnight, the mechanics of paying for computation changed: every block now included a protocol-set *base fee* that would be burned, while users attached a *tip* to compete for priority. The auction rules changed. This was not a tweak to user experience; it was a reallocation of bargaining power between transactors and validators, and a structural statement about who should capture the value of congestion. Within hours, explorers displayed flames beside transactions as fees were destroyed, and dashboards tracked how much ether was being burned. Monetary effects drew headlines. The deeper shift lay elsewhere: Ethereum had admitted, in code, that blockspace is not a neutral pipe but a rationed market. How that market is designed decides whose transactions clear, whose strategies win, and whose assumptions about fairness survive contact with software.

Show → Name → Explain → Implication. The show is familiar to anyone who lived through December 2017 when CryptoKitties clogged the chain: pending transactions stacked up, gas prices spiked, and ordinary transfers waited behind speculative bids for feline DNA. Name it: congestion. Explain: a globally shared computer has finite execution capacity per block; when demand exceeds that capacity, users enter an auction for inclusion. Implication: if you do not choose auction rules explicitly, you inherit them implicitly—and the winners will be those best equipped to game them. Ethereum's politics begins here, not in forums but in mempools.

EIP-1559 reframed the auction. Previously, users guessed a gas price and hoped miners would include their transaction; underpricing meant getting stuck, overpricing meant overpaying. The new mechanism separates two questions: *How much must everyone pay to enter?* (the base fee, adjusting block by block), and *Who should go first?* (the tip, a small premium). This structure reduces guesswork and cushions price shocks by making the base fee responsive to demand. Burning the base fee also redirects a portion of congestion rent away from validators and into scarcity shared by all ether holders. The implication is constitutional: fee design is not merely UX; it is a distributional choice about who captures the value of blockspace scarcity.

But the auction has a shadow market. In 2019, researchers highlighted "Flash Boys 2.0": strategies by which sophisticated actors profit by reordering, inserting, or censoring transactions within a block—*miner/maximum extractable value* (MEV). Show the practice: an arbitrageur front-runs a large trade, a liquidator snipes an undercollateralised loan, a sandwich attack brackets a user's swap to extract rent. Name it: MEV. Explain: some sequences of transactions are more profitable than others; whoever controls ordering can harvest the difference. Implication: if the protocol does not constrain ordering, a second auction emerges—off-chain and invisible to regular users—where searchers pay validators (or their delegates) for the right to insert their bundles in a particular position.

Ethereum's response since the Merge (September 2022) has been pragmatic and political. Pragmatic, because the protocol embraced *proposer–builder separation* (PBS) in practice via MEV-Boost relays, allowing specialised builders to assemble high-value blocks while validators simply choose the best bid. Political, because this structure formalised a new layer of intermediation in the block production pipeline. Show: validators run MEV-Boost; builders compete to supply them with blocks; relays route bundles. Name: MEV-Boost, Flashbots. Explain: separating roles aims to reduce centralising pressure on validators by letting them outsource complex optimisation to builders while still capturing revenue. Implication: fairness now depends not only on base fees and tips, but on who has access to builder markets, which private order flows they receive, and what policies relays enforce.

Fairness in blockspace is therefore not an abstract virtue but a measurable set of behaviours. Who clears first when gas spikes? Which transactions are systematically sandwiched? How much of validator revenue comes from MEV versus tips and issuance? Exchanges adjust confirmation times when volatility rises; wallets adjust default fees; protocols change parameters to withstand liquidation cascades. Each decision reveals how the market perceives risk. In May 2020, when Uniswap v2 launched automated markets that could be arbitraged continuously, bots began bidding for priority in *priority gas auctions*; in March 2020's "Black Thursday", MakerDAO liquidations clustered behind soaring gas costs and mempool instability. The lesson is consistent: when blockspace tightens, power moves to those who can price latency, pre-commit capital, and maintain privileged routes to builders.

The first named, checkable example of how economic design alters distribution is again EIP-1559. Post-upgrade, users typically specify a *max fee* and a *priority tip*. Under normal conditions, wallets can guide users toward efficient settings, reducing the "auction anxiety" that previously led to chronic overpayment. Meanwhile, the burning of base fees changes the long-run supply dynamics of ether and, indirectly, validator incentives: when price appreciation is tied partly to network demand, validators' private rent capture faces a counterweight from the public. The implication is subtle: a monetary burn does not fix congestion, but it shifts the politics of who benefits from it.

A second example is the rise of *private RPCs* and *order flow auctions*. Major wallets and decentralised exchanges now route transactions to private endpoints that bypass the public mempool, promising protection from sandwich attacks and offering users a share of the MEV rebates that their order flow generates. Show: a wallet toggles "private" mode; transactions skip the gossip layer; builders compete to include the bundle; the user receives a small rebate. Name: private order flow, flow auctions. Explain: by internalising the value of order flow and constraining public visibility, wallets attempt to protect retail users while monetising their position in the pipeline. Implication: protections improve for those inside curated corridors; externalities increase for those outside. Access becomes a policy decision embedded in software defaults.

The credible counter-example to protocol-level rationing as a fairness tool is to expand capacity—make blocks much bigger or move most activity off the base chain. Networks like Solana pursue high throughput and low fees by design; Ethereum itself encourages rollups to absorb the mass of transactions and post compressed proofs on L1. This works, up to a point. Wider pipes relieve pressure. But they do not abolish auctions. High-throughput chains still see MEV contests around liquidations and arbitrage; rollups inherit ordering games within their own sequencers, and cross-domain MEV emerges wherever bridges and shared assets interlock. The reconciliation is pragmatic: capacity buys time; design decides who benefits from that time. Even in abundance, blockspace is not free; it is merely cheaper to compete for.

Return to the motif that will guide the remainder of this subchapter: *Who gets the front of the queue?* The queue is the mempool (or its private equivalents). The front is an ordered list chosen by a validator or builder. The answer is never "everyone equally"; it is always "those who priced the moment correctly, or those whose transactions travel privileged lanes". Policy lives in defaults. A wallet that overestimates tips during congestion protects users at the cost of overpaying; a protocol that batches withdrawals reduces per-user fees but increases burstiness; a relay that excludes certain bundles for compliance reasons shifts extraction to other venues or induces censorship risk. Each behavior is a decision about fairness translated into code.

Ethereum's fee market sits at the intersection of three incentives: users want inclusion at predictable cost; validators want revenue with minimal variance; the network wants decentralisation and liveness. MEV complicates all three. For users, the presence of searchers means some trades will remain systematically disadvantaged without protection; for validators, outsourcing to builders maximises income but may concentrate power in a few sophisticated firms; for the network, the emergence of private order flow threatens the ideal of a common mempool by fragmenting information. The implication is not that MEV is optional; it is that MEV must be governed—or at least channelled—by economic design that acknowledges these trade-offs.

Consider two further, grounded examples that measure design against outcome. After the Merge, validator revenue regularly displayed three components on public dashboards: issuance (now minimal under proof-of-stake), tips, and MEV-Boost payments. During periods of intense activity—NFT drops such as Yuga Labs' Otherside mint in April 2022 on pre-Merge PoW, and subsequent L2 surges—MEV-related payments formed a meaningful share of income. Validators behaved accordingly: those who did not run MEV-Boost left money on the table. The implication is behavioural, not moral: when the protocol allows value extraction, actors who refuse to participate subsidise those who do. Designing for equity therefore requires either narrowing the channels for extraction or broadening access to them.

Next, look at rollups. Arbitrum and Optimism introduced sequencers that order transactions within their domains. Today, these sequencers are typically centralised or semi-centralised. They can mitigate retail harm by implementing fair-ordering policies or private matching, but they also represent new choke points and new auctions for preferential inclusion. Measurable behaviours—latency to L1 posting, frequency of reorgs on L2, presence of reordering around large swaps—tell us whether the fairness promised at L2 translates into practice. The implication is systemic: blockspace is now multi-tiered. Political economy migrates *up* the stack, not away.

A fair fee market is not one without pain; it is one where pain is predictable, contestable, and not monopolised by insiders. Predictability comes from mechanisms like EIP-1559 that make base costs legible. Contestability comes from open access to builder markets and from research into protocol-enforced PBS that reduces reliance on private relays. Non-monopolisation comes from client diversity, validator set dispersion, and wallet defaults that do not quietly tax naïve order flow. Each aim has metrics. Base fee volatility can be measured; builder concentration can be tracked by share of winning bids; client diversity is visible in consensus client distribution; wallet behaviours can be audited by comparing outcomes for "protected" versus public submissions. What gets measured gets governed.

There is a harder edge to the fairness debate: censorship. In August 2022, when a prominent mixer was sanctioned by the U.S. Treasury, some relays and builders chose to filter transactions interacting with those addresses. Validators connected only to those relays unwittingly produced "compliant" blocks. The behaviour was visible on chain: a non-trivial proportion of blocks for a period excluded certain flows. Whatever one's view of the policy, the technical implication was clear. If a small set of relays dominates, policy risk concentrates. The remedy is pluralism: more relays, open-source relay software, and—longer-term—protocol-level PBS that reduces reliance on intermediaries susceptible to regulatory capture.

The counter-example to despair is equally real: *public goods hardening*. Research communities, grant programmes, and client teams have steadily chipped away at the worst externalities. Better mempool simulations have reduced fee guesswork; wallets integrate on-chain data to suggest realistic tips; some builders commit to transparent policies; community pressure has kept client monocultures from taking hold. None of this abolishes the queue. It makes the queue less arbitrary.

We can now state the diagnostic questions that will recur throughout the chapter. When gas spikes, who consistently clears first—and why? When MEV rises, who captures it—validators, builders, wallets, or protected users? When relays change policies, how quickly can validators route around them? When a rollup's sequencer misbehaves, how costly is exit to L1? Each answer converts sentiment into structure. It reveals where fairness lives, and where it merely gestures.

The motif returns for the last time. Who gets the front of the queue? A free-for-all is not fair; a cartel is not fair; a market with transparent rules and plural access can be. Ethereum's evolution since EIP-1559 and the Merge has been an attempt to write those rules without destroying the incentives that keep the machine running. Whether it succeeds will be decided not by rhetoric but by routine: which defaults wallets choose, which relays validators trust, which fee policies clients implement, which protections become norms. The unresolved test stands. How much opacity will we tolerate to protect users from predators, and how much openness will we risk to keep the queue common? Economic design cannot please everyone. It can, with discipline, refuse to privilege the few.

Upgrades as Constitutional Moments

At 06:42:42 UTC on 15 September 2022, Ethereum changed its mind without losing its memory. The network finalised a block under proof-of-stake for the first time—the culmination of a long-promised transition known as the Merge. No mint paused. No balances vanished. Block time held steady. Terminal Total Difficulty was reached; clients switched consensus; validators proposed, attested, and finalised. The lights stayed on. This was not a patch; it was a constitutional rewrite conducted under load. The code took precedence today. Yet what made the event credible was not only software but the social process that made the rewrite legitimate.

The Merge offers a clean lens for this subchapter's claim: major upgrades in programmable ledgers act like constitutional amendments. They reallocate rights, responsibilities, and rewards. They must therefore pass a higher bar than ordinary engineering. Their legitimacy depends on three tests that will serve as our motif: *sunlight, dissent, exit.* Sunlight asks whether the change is visible and intelligible before it binds. Dissent asks whether minority views can be aired, organised, and survive. Exit asks whether those who reject the rewrite retain a viable path, technical and economic, to continue under old rules. The strength of a ledger's constitution is measured not in its rhetoric but in these behaviours.

Show → Name → Explain → Implication. The Merge shows how sunlight works in a decentralised system. Name the apparatus: public AllCoreDevs calls; client-team design notes; open repositories; shadow forks; merge testnets; a well-advertised activation condition (TTD). Explain the mechanism: the network rehearsed its amendment in the open, on repeated dress rehearsals, with multiple independent teams implementing the same specification. Users could watch releases, read breaking changes, and measure readiness by the presence—or absence—of updated binaries in the wild. Implication: transparency converts risk into informed consent. When a protocol alters who secures it and how, the path to change must itself be legible.

Dissent next. The Merge retired proof-of-work. Some miners refused. A faction launched EthereumPoW, preserving mining and creating a forked asset. Exchanges listed, then liquidity and attention thinned. The majority did not punish dissent; it priced it. Validators on the main chain continued; the minority exercised the constitutional right to depart. Implication: an amendment gains legitimacy not by preventing dissent but by surviving it without coercion. Dissent that can exit is safer than dissent that must sabotage.

Exit last. The weeks around the Merge made exit operable rather than theoretical. Replay protection, distinct chain identifiers, and explicit signalling by client teams and exchanges ensured that those who did not agree could keep a consistent history without polluting the other. The market answered the political question. One chain's security and economic activity dwarfed the other's, but the choice remained real. Implication: a constitution worthy of the name must allow lawful loss. If the only way to object is to crash the system, there is no constitution—only a truce.

A second case anchors the motif in economic design: the London upgrade on 5 August 2021, which introduced EIP-1559. Sunlight was relentless. The proposal evolved through months of public debate; researchers modelled fee dynamics; wallets trialled user flows; miners and pools publicly signalled opposition, then adapted. The behaviour was measurable on day one: blocks burned base fees; users attached tips; fee volatility dropped relative to the pre-London blind auction. The politics sits in the burn. By destroying the base fee, London redirected a share of congestion rent away from block producers and towards all ether holders. That was a shift in distributive power, not just UX. Legitimacy turned on whether the community accepted the *why* as well as the *how*. It did. Not unanimously. Enough.

Legitimacy also has a stern face: knowing when not to rewrite. In November 2017, a bug in the Parity multisig library froze hundreds of wallets, trapping a large sum of ether beyond recovery. Aggrieved projects argued for a special-purpose hard fork. Developers discussed options in public. No amendment came. Sunlight was present; dissent was heard; exit was inapplicable because the request was to change the past on the canonical chain. The constitution held by refusing exceptional relief. Implication: amendment restraint is as formative as amendment success. A ledger that rewrites for private loss trains its citizenry to politicise every failure.

The canonical constitutional drama remains the DAO fork of July 2016. The chain rewrote a narrow slice of history to undo the consequences of a vulnerability that had diverted funds. The dissent was principled; the exit was real. Ethereum Classic emerged as a standing reminder that minorities should not need permission to keep the old rules. The lesson is not that one side was right and the other wrong. It is that a constitution was born in the act—sunlight through weeks of debate; dissent articulated by named maintainers and miners; exit formalised in code and markets. Each subsequent amendment lives in its shadow.

These cases clarify the anatomy of an upgrade as a constitutional moment. First, amendment proposals must be more than code diffs; they are *arguments*. EIPs and research posts are parliamentary records for a stateless polity. Their quality matters. Vague justifications corrode trust; clear trade-offs earn it. The Merge's choice of Terminal Total Difficulty, rather than a calendar date, embedded a principle: the network should turn when the system itself demonstrates readiness, not when leaders decree it. The behaviour is the principle.

Second, the social infrastructure must make dissent cheap. Cheap dissent produces honest signal. Mailing lists, public calls, independent client teams, and alternative implementations allow disagreement without sabotage. In the run-up to London, miner groups proposed "show-of-hashpower" protests; some blocks included empty payloads to display displeasure. The network did not retaliate; it endured. That forbearance is a constitutional asset. A polity that punishes peaceful protest gets violent protest.

Third, exit must be technically straightforward and economically costly in a way that markets—not gatekeepers—determine. The machinery here is mundane and vital: chain IDs that prevent replay, seeding mechanisms for bootstrap peers, documented differences, and a clear commitment by exchanges and custodians to let markets clear the question of salience. The DAO split rehearsed this. The Merge renewed it. A constitution that condemns exit to chaos tempts exit by sabotage.

Constitutional moments also involve quieter, administrative choices that shape power for years. Shanghai/Capella in April 2023, which enabled withdrawals for staked ether, is a case in point. It did not only release liquidity; it matured the political economy of staking by making entry and exit credible. The signal was visible in validator behaviour: more voluntary exits at the margin; more churn management by the protocol; more dispersion of staking across providers once lock-in fear waned. The amendment encoded a promise: capital cannot be conscripted indefinitely. Legitimacy increased because exit became routine.

A credible counter-argument runs like this: frequent constitutional change risks turning a settlement layer into a perpetual motion machine of politics. If rules are always under revision, how can contracts trust the ground beneath them? The critique is not frivolous. The reconciliation rests on cadence and scope. Ethereum's most consequential amendments sit on multi-year horizons, with aggressive testing and clear activation criteria; smaller, reversible changes iterate at the edges. The distinction is moral as much as technical. Constitutional amendments should *simplify* the core, harden guarantees, or repair existential flaws. Feature accretion belongs elsewhere. When amendments become feature lists, legitimacy thins.

The motif returns: sunlight, dissent, exit. Each has metrics. Sunlight can be measured by lead time between specification and activation, by the number and independence of implementations, by the readability of change logs and the availability of testnets. Dissent can be measured by participation in public calls, by the diversity of objections, by the presence of minority client teams willing to say no. Exit can be measured by the practical feasibility of running an alternative network, by the speed with which chain IDs and replay protection appear, by the willingness of exchanges to list and let markets speak. These are not abstract virtues. They are behaviours a careful observer can document.

Legitimacy also depends on who is *absent* from the room. Client monocultures concentrate risk; single points of interpretive authority concentrate power. The Merge succeeded in part because no one team could credibly act alone. Prysm, Lighthouse, Teku, Nimbus, and others each carried part of the load. Diversity was not decoration; it was constitutional ballast. The same is true for execution clients and for the ecosystem of auditors, researchers, and tooling teams that shape the rough consensus of a global developer polity. A constitution is a choreography, not a command.

Even constitutional triumphs leave residua. The advent of MEV-Boost relays in the Merge's wake created new chokepoints where policy could bite. For a time, some relays filtered sanctioned flows; validators connected only to those relays produced blocks that reflected those policies. Sunlight, dissent, exit again: public dashboards displayed relay shares and policies; validators debated and diversified; alternative relays and strategies emerged; protocol-level proposer–builder separation is under study to reduce reliance on intermediaries. The constitutional work continues after the amendment, because each amendment shifts the field on which the next questions will be contested.

Where the analogy to constitutions bites hardest is in what happens when things go wrong under pressure. September 2016 taught that "code is law" is an incomplete sentence; January 2019's last-minute delay of the Constantinople upgrade after a late-discovered vulnerability taught that "law must wait for safety". In each case, public process turned embarrassment into legitimacy by narrating the choice. Clients delayed. Exchanges paused. Coordination costs were paid in daylight. A state without state still governs by explanation.

The forward test is stark. How should a programmable ledger decide when to use its amendment power to confront threats that are partly technical and partly political—censorship at relays, concentration in staking, cross-domain MEV that undermines fairness? Who has standing to veto an amendment, and on what grounds? How much exit can a system tolerate before shared liquidity and composability fracture? The constitution lives in those questions, not in slogans.

One more time: sunlight, dissent, exit. A ledger that passes those tests turns upgrades into a source of strength rather than a source of fear. A ledger that fails them will find that its boldest code cannot redeem a broken process. The next amendment will arrive. It will redistribute something that matters. When it does, who will illuminate it, who will object without being punished, and who will walk away without burning the house?

Composability and Cascade Risk

On 12 March 2020, as global markets lurched, Ethereum gas prices spiked and MakerDAO's liquidation auctions jammed. Keepers who usually bid to buy collateral found their transactions stuck; some bids cleared at effectively zero because congestion starved competitors of inclusion. By the end of that week in London and everywhere else the network touched, borrowers had lost collateral not to superior price discovery but to clogged pipes. The contracts behaved as coded. The system behaved as a system. One protocol's stress metastasised into others through shared liquidity, shared oracles, and shared blockspace. The Lego metaphor looked less like play and more like scaffolding under wind load. It bent.

DeFi's promise rests on composability: contracts that call contracts, money legos snapping together to create markets, treasuries, and institutions at software speed. The same property engineers love is the one risk managers fear. Connections multiply function; connections multiply failure. The motif that will guide this subchapter is the *load-bearing join*—the hinge that makes two bricks useful and also makes them jointly fragile. Each time we celebrate a neat join—an AMM plugged into a lending pool, a price oracle wired to a stablecoin minter—we should ask the boring questions. Where does the join fail? Who depends on it? How quickly can it be repaired under congestion?

Show → Name → Explain → Implication. Begin with the MakerDAO "Black Thursday" episode. Show: gas surged, keepers timed out, and auctions cleared at non-competitive prices. Name: MakerDAO liquidations, 12–13 March 2020. Explain: liquidation engines assumed a functioning mempool and diverse bidders; under stress, the assumption broke. A single protocol's dependency on external keepers and blockspace liquidity converted volatility into insolvency risk. Implication: a protocol is only as resilient as the slowest actor in its critical path. If the chain can't breathe, none of the bricks can stand.

A second example, precise and checkable, arrived on 30 July 2023 when a compiler bug in certain Vyper versions opened Curve Finance pools to re-entrancy. Show: a flaw in code libraries used by multiple pools enabled draining; liquidity fled to safer venues; governance tokens sold off; protocols downstream that had used Curve LP tokens as collateral scrambled to raise thresholds and pause riskier markets. Name: the Curve/Vyper re-entrancy incident. Explain: "shared components" are shared failure domains; when many bricks use the same joint, one crack stresses the wall. Implication: composability amplifies correlated risk; audit diversity and dependency maps matter as much as any single contract's formal proof.

The counter-example that tempers fatalism is real and instructive. When staked-Ether (stETH) traded at a discount to Ether in June 2022, lending protocols such as Aave adjusted collateral factors and liquidation parameters quickly; large liquidations were absorbed without a death spiral. Show: governance forums posted proposals; risk teams modelled scenarios; parameters changed within hours or days; liquidations cleared at live prices with functioning oracles. Name: the stETH de-peg stress and Aave/Maker responses. Explain: not all joins are brittle; where dependency and response paths were mapped in advance—with bounded oracle delays, circuit breakers, and pre-authorised risk teams—contagion was contained. Implication: composability can be disciplined; it requires routine drills, not hope.

Correlated failure in DeFi hides in plain sight. It lives in oracle design, in the geographic and client diversity of keepers, in the concentration of liquidity, in bridges that turn two security models into one shared blast radius, and in governance shortcuts that concentrate emergency power in five keys on one multisig. Pair each abstraction with its behaviour. *Trust* is the oracle update interval measured in blocks and the mix of data sources; *efficiency* is the p95 time-to-finality under congestion, not the average; *risk* is the share of a protocol's collateral that maps to a single asset, chain, or price feed; *resilience* is the existence of a pause that can be invoked by more than a cosy quorum and less than a mob.

The join where oracles meet markets is the first hinge to test. Price feeds are not divine truths; they are sampled views. Protocols that leaned too heavily on time-weighted on-chain prices discovered how manipulable those can be on thin liquidity. The bZx exploits of 2020, for example, stitched together flash loans and AMM price influence to game collateral valuation. The better pattern that has emerged mixes sources (robust off-chain reporters, thick on-chain references, bounded deviation checks) and gates consumption (slippage-aware liquidation engines, delayed acceptance of extreme moves, and circuit breakers that halt if price oracles diverge beyond a threshold). The implication is simple: an oracle that updates quickly aids fairness during calm and invites manipulation during turbulence. The hinge must flex only within defined ranges.

The second hinge is liquidity dependence. Lending protocols often accept LP tokens as collateral; yield aggregators farm those same pools; treasuries post the same baskets in multiple venues. The result is a loop: a shock to pool health degrades collateral quality, which triggers liquidations that drain the same pool, which worsens prices, and so on. The behaviour is measurable: a rising share of protocol TVL concentrated in the top two or three pools; cross-holdings revealed in governance dashboards; liquidation volumes peaking as AMM depth thins. A stress-test worth running before crisis is this: assume the largest pool's depth halves at the same time as gas doubles and oracle delays widen. Can your liquidations still clear without cascading? If not, the Lego tower is taller than its base.

Bridges form a third hinge—glamorous when they work, catastrophic when they fail. The 2022 Wormhole exploit, though on a different chain, illustrated a general truth: when a bridge mints wrapped assets against claims on a remote chain, the wrapped assets' validity depends on the weakest link in a complex path of signatures, relayers, guardians, and contracts. The implication for composability on Ethereum is immediate. If your protocol accepts bridged assets as collateral, your true collateral is the bridge. Your stress-test is not complete until you model the cost and dynamics of a remote failure, the pause paths on both sides, and the time to "light-switch" assets out of collateral sets with minimal governance friction.

MEV and mempool dynamics create a fourth hinge by turning time into an adversary. A liquidation engine that assumes it will win the race to submit the best transaction collides with builders and searchers whose sole aim is to out-order it. The behaviour during stress is visible: liquidations cluster in blocks that also host arbitrage bundles; keepers who cannot pay for priority lose to those who can; user transactions languish until the liquidation storm subsides. The implication: your resilience is not your algorithm's elegance; it is your access to the front of the queue. A credible test is to simulate liquidations with order-flow protection disabled and gas two standard deviations above recent medians. If performance collapses, your system depends on privileged lanes rather than robust design.

Governance is the quietest hinge and often the most dangerous. Emergency pause powers centralised in a three-of-five multisig give comfort until one signer is unreachable, one is compromised, and one is asleep. Timelocks that protect against rushed, malicious upgrades become liabilities when you need to deploy a critical fix under active exploitation. The behaviour that separates mature systems from improv theatre is mundane: clearly documented authority for emergency teams; multi-stage pause modes (from "halt just a market" to "halt protocol-wide"); procedures for rapid oracle substitution; and post-mortems that commit to rewiring the hinge rather than retelling the story. The implication: composability without governance choreography is not decentralisation; it is delegation to the nearest adults in the room.

So what does a *stress-test checklist* look like when we refuse bullet points and insist on behaviours? It looks like a dry run in which a protocol team commits to measurable drills. Map every upstream and downstream dependency—price feeds, bridges, LP tokens, keeper fleets, relays, builders—and assign a failure mode and a response time to each. Measure liquidation throughput not in lab conditions but with mainnet-level noise injected: reorderings, delayed blocks, temporarily censored flows through a dominant relay. Commit, in advance, to conservative parameter ranges that trip automatically: LTV caps that tighten when oracle deviations widen; fee multipliers that rise when mempools bloat; caps on collateral types that self-enforce when any single asset breaches a concentration threshold. Require proof of disperse keepers: not a count of bots, but an audit of their clients, geographies, and order-flow routes. Insist that every "pause" is paired with a "resume": who can restart, on what evidence, with what quorum, and after what cool-down? Then rehearse the drill with real money at the margin: small auctions, partial pauses, staged restarts. You do not own resilience until you have paid for it with foregone yield.

Two further named episodes sharpen this discipline. First, the post-Merge rise of private order-flow auctions and MEV-Boost relays created new public-goods questions. Some relays briefly filtered sanctioned addresses in late 2022; validators that connected only to those relays produced selectively censored blocks. Teams that had assumed neutral ordering found themselves exposed to policy choices made far away. The operational fix—connecting to multiple relays, supporting diverse clients, and monitoring relay shares—became part of responsible deployment. Second, the April 2023 Shanghai/Capella upgrade, by enabling withdrawals, changed staking dynamics and the composition of "safe" collateral across protocols. Risk teams that modelled validator exit churn and the knock-on effects on staking derivatives coped; those who treated staked assets as static found their assumptions evaporating. In both cases, the *join* had moved; only those who kept the map up to date avoided surprises.

A credible limitation must be admitted. Over-caution can smother innovation. Parameter hair-triggering can trigger needless pauses; conservative collateral sets can concentrate risk elsewhere; overly broad circuit breakers can hand adversaries new griefing tools. The reconciliation is to treat stress-testing as a scalpel, not a blanket. Design thresholds that scale with volatility regimes; prefer market-specific halts to protocol-wide freezes; privilege automatic, localised responses over social-layer heroics. Most of all, publish your drills. Sunlight is not just a virtue; it is a deterrent. Adversaries read documentation too.

The motif returns: the load-bearing join. Think of oracles, bridges, mempools, governance keys, and liquidity pools as hinges rather than bricks. Hinges need lubrication, inspection, and redundancy; they also need limits on load. If a hinge is rated for a certain weight, you either lighten the wall or add another hinge. Translated: cap collateral concentrations; diversify oracle sources; split pause powers; secure access to multiple order-flow routes; treat bridged assets as second-class collateral unless and until bridge guarantees approach those of the base layer.

The forward test is not whether a single contract has been audited to virtue; it is whether a protocol's *connections* have been rehearsed to failure. Teams should invite third parties to stress specific joins: block builders who simulate re-ordering; oracle providers who induce safe deviations; white-hat keepers who race each other under fee storms; bridge operators who stage test failures that propagate wrapped assets as "suspect" and watch downstream protocols react. The question that matters is painfully simple: when the hinge groans, does the wall hold long enough for someone to redistribute weight?

Composability is DeFi's genius. It is also its correlation engine. The only honest safety lies in treating the network like an unfinished building: always occupied, always being renovated, and always at risk where one piece meets another. The next shock will not arrive where you looked last; it will traverse the join you forgot to test. Are you mapping it now—or will you learn its shape in the dark?

Chapter 4
Central Bank Digital Currencies: Control, Care, or Both?

On 4 October 2020, in Shenzhen, the People's Bank of China launched its first public pilot of the digital yuan. Ten million citizens received small allocations of the new currency, distributed by lottery and spendable through state-linked wallets. Payments cleared instantly; balances sat directly on a central ledger. The spectacle was not about speed or novelty—it was about control. Every yuan could be traced, every transaction could be programmed. For the first time since banknotes replaced silver, money itself had gained conditions. The experiment's subtext was global: if a state can re-engineer cash, what else can it rewrite?

Central bank digital currencies—CBDCs—are not simply the next step in monetary technology; they are a fork in monetary philosophy. They ask whether the instrument of exchange should become an instrument of policy execution. To some, they promise a safer, more inclusive financial architecture where trust is restored through direct public money. To others, they are the most refined surveillance tool ever conceived, the fusion of fiscal policy, identity systems, and code. The question is not whether governments *can* issue programmable money, but whether they *should*—and, if they do, who will guard the guardians of the ledger?

What a CBDC *is* can be defined cleanly enough in the language of liabilities: it is central bank money in digital form, distinct from commercial bank deposits or crypto assets because it is a direct claim on the state, not a derivative of one. Yet what a CBDC *does*—and what it *means*—depends on design. Does it settle instantly, like cash, or through intermediaries like existing payment rails? Does it mimic the privacy of notes or the audit trail of banking apps? Does it allow a government to distribute emergency relief at speed, or to switch off dissenters with a line of code? Every architectural decision carries political freight disguised as technical necessity.

The appeal to central bankers is understandable. Since 2008, faith in transmission—the way policy rates move through the financial system—has frayed. Negative rates and quantitative easing flooded balance sheets but rarely reached the citizen. A retail CBDC offers the prospect of direct channels: programmable stimulus, automatic tax collection, conditional spending to nudge consumption. The narrative is one of *care*: inclusion for the unbanked, efficiency for the system, responsiveness for policy. But the same levers can enforce discipline. A line between *care* and *control* runs through the code itself.

Programmability is the hinge of this debate. A CBDC that can enforce spending limits, expiry dates, or sectoral restrictions turns monetary policy into behavioural policy. In the aftermath of the pandemic, when central banks discussed "helicopter money" and targeted support, programmable features seemed pragmatic. Yet each function has a fine print of freedom. Who defines legitimate use? Who audits conditions attached to transactions? Can users opt out of algorithmic compliance? The question of auditability extends beyond accounting: in a programmable currency, freedom survives only as long as its conditions are contestable.

Architecture amplifies the moral stakes. A *wholesale* CBDC, accessible only to banks and financial institutions, refines plumbing; a *retail* CBDC, accessible to everyone, reshapes sovereignty. The intermediated model—favoured by the European Central Bank and the Bank of England—preserves private banks as conduits for wallet interfaces while anchoring the base ledger at the central bank. It promises resilience through redundancy. Yet intermediated systems inherit the vulnerabilities of the old world: outages, privacy leaks, and corporate gatekeepers. Direct retail models, as tested in the Bahamas' Sand Dollar and Nigeria's eNaira, eliminate those layers at the cost of political intimacy: every citizen becomes a customer of the central bank. A programmable wallet in the pocket is a political act disguised as convenience.

Privacy, long treated as a consumer choice, becomes a constitutional principle under CBDCs. Physical cash embodies anonymity by default; digital money reverses the presumption. The Bank for International Settlements speaks of "controlled anonymity", an artful phrase that translates as *privacy until the state requires otherwise.*

The European Central Bank's prototypes speak of "tiered privacy" and "anonymity vouchers"—metaphors that reveal the dilemma: freedom rationed by design. Even China, whose digital yuan allows programmable visibility to varying degrees, has had to reassure the public that "full traceability" will be "reasonably limited". The credibility of such assurances will decide whether digital money feels like a right or a leash.

Geopolitics shadows every domestic debate. Cross-border payment networks, once dull infrastructure, have become instruments of foreign policy. The SWIFT exclusions of 2022 showed how easily the global settlement system could be weaponised. In response, multiple states began experimenting with sovereign rails—Russia's SPFS, China's CIPS, and now CBDC corridors linking BRICS nations. A digital yuan that clears in Shanghai or a digital rupee that settles in Mumbai bypasses Western-controlled intermediaries and, by extension, Western leverage. CBDCs are thus not only about payments but about *position*: who defines compliance, whose laws apply, and whose surveillance reaches where. The pipes of money are fast becoming the frontlines of sovereignty.

At the same time, CBDCs could, paradoxically, reinforce global standards. A universally interoperable design could reduce the friction of remittances, lower costs for migrants, and increase transparency in cross-border trade. The same features that frighten privacy advocates—traceability, programmability, enforcement—could deter corruption and fraud when applied judiciously. Whether they serve openness or isolation will depend less on code than on governance. As one senior central banker remarked privately, "The technology is neutral; the policy is not."

Every civilisation has had its signature medium of trust: clay tokens, silver coins, paper notes, electronic balances. Each medium encoded a balance of power between the state, the citizen, and the market. CBDCs are the first to fuse that balance into a programmable substrate. They collapse the distance between issuing authority and end-user, between monetary design and social design. The question before policymakers and publics alike is deceptively simple: when money itself can carry instructions, what instructions do we accept—and from whom?

The chapter that follows examines that question across four dimensions. It defines CBDCs by their liabilities and limits, distinguishing them from the private credit money of banks and the anarchic freedom of cryptocurrencies. It explores programmability as both opportunity and hazard, a tool that can deliver targeted welfare or subtle coercion. It dissects the architectural choices—retail, wholesale, and intermediated—that determine privacy, resilience, and the survival of commercial banking as we know it. And it places CBDCs in their geopolitical context, as instruments of competition and cooperation on the new frontier of digital settlement.

The motif running through these pages is the *paradox of proximity*: the closer money comes to its issuer, the more it reveals about the kind of state behind it. A CBDC can express care through inclusion, or control through inspection. It can widen participation or tighten compliance. The code will not decide; the constitution behind the code will. And that, more than the technology itself, will tell us whether the next monetary revolution delivers liberation—or obedience.

What a CBDC Is—and Isn't

In February 2023, Christine Lagarde, President of the European Central Bank, stood before the European Parliament in Strasbourg and described the proposed digital euro as "a complement, not a replacement" for cash. Her phrasing was deliberate. The project's supporters were anxious to separate digital central bank money from both commercial bank deposits and the volatile world of crypto assets. Yet beneath the cautious rhetoric was an audacious claim: that the state could re-engineer money itself—preserving trust while modernising its machinery. A Central Bank Digital Currency (CBDC) would not just update the plumbing of payments; it would redefine what it means to hold a public claim on a sovereign institution in an age when most "money" exists as private credit.

To understand the ambition, one must start with the balance sheet. A CBDC, like a banknote, is a direct liability of the central bank. A commercial bank deposit, by contrast, is a liability of a private institution, backed by reserves and confidence. The distinction sounds technical but is constitutional: one is risk-free because it is the state's promise; the other is risk-managed because it is the market's. When you hold cash, you hold a public guarantee. When you hold a deposit, you hold a promise that the guarantee will be honoured *through* intermediaries. A CBDC collapses this hierarchy. It brings citizens back into direct relationship with the sovereign balance sheet—digitally, instantly, and, potentially, programmably.

That directness carries both clarity and danger. In the conventional system, central bank money forms the foundation upon which private credit money is multiplied through lending. The two tiers—state and bank—balance efficiency with stability. Banks create most of the money supply through deposits and loans, while central banks anchor trust through reserves and settlement. A retail CBDC would blur this separation. If citizens could hold electronic central bank money directly, they might prefer it to bank deposits during stress, draining liquidity from the private sector. The very safety that makes CBDCs appealing could, if mishandled, destabilise the banking system they are meant to support.

China's digital yuan, piloted since 2020 by the People's Bank of China, illustrates both the potential and the peril. Officially, the system mirrors cash: a "two-tier" model where banks distribute central bank money to users. In practice, the digital yuan ledger sits under direct state oversight. Balances can expire, transactions can be tracked, and programmable features enable targeted transfers. These are not theoretical possibilities; they have been demonstrated in pilot cities such as Shenzhen and Suzhou. The architecture delivers efficiency and fine-grained policy control, but it also places citizens one software update away from conditional spending. The project is not merely technological—it is ideological. It treats money as a policy instrument first, a public medium second.

Contrast this with the Swedish e-krona project, where the Riksbank—confronting the world's fastest decline in cash usage—has tested a CBDC designed to preserve the *character* of cash, including offline functionality and pseudonymous small-value transactions. The intent is inclusion rather than command. In both cases, design expresses philosophy: who issues, who intermediates, who can see. The same technology can produce very different constitutional outcomes.

Liability defines a CBDC's nature; *settlement* defines its function. Commercial bank payments rely on layered reconciliation—an IOU chain settled at intervals through the central bank's real-time gross settlement (RTGS) system. Crypto assets, by contrast, settle directly on their own ledgers, with finality probabilistic and decentralised. A CBDC occupies a middle ground: state-guaranteed finality, achieved digitally, without the probabilistic lag of proof-of-work or the dependency of correspondent banking. For central bankers, this is not about competing with Bitcoin's ideology but about defending their own relevance. A CBDC ensures that public money—long confined to interbank reserves—remains a living instrument in an age of private digital rails.

Yet programmability introduces a third dimension, beyond liability and settlement: *intent.* Money that carries code carries policy. The Bank of England's consultation on a digital pound (2023) explicitly entertained "conditional payments" to enable welfare disbursement, green incentives, or targeted tax rebates. Each function appears benign; collectively they redefine monetary neutrality. A payment instrument that can discriminate by purpose or recipient is no longer a neutral unit of account—it becomes a conduit of governance. The political question is buried in the syntax of smart contracts: who writes the conditions, who audits them, and what recourse exists if they misfire?

The promise of inclusion drives much of the official enthusiasm. The Bank for International Settlements (BIS) has framed CBDCs as tools to "leave no one behind" in an increasingly cashless economy. In theory, a digital form of public money could reach unbanked citizens without relying on profit-seeking intermediaries. In practice, access depends on infrastructure—devices, connectivity, and digital identity systems that often exclude the very groups the policy aims to serve. The Nigerian eNaira, launched in October 2021, exemplifies this paradox. Despite government backing, adoption lagged: by early 2023, less than one per cent of Nigerians had used it regularly. Trust, not technology, proved decisive. People preferred familiar mobile money services run by private firms. The state could issue a token, but it could not compel belief.

Efficiency is the second great promise. Traditional payment systems rely on a lattice of intermediaries—clearing houses, card networks, correspondent banks—each taking a fee and introducing latency. CBDCs could, in principle, collapse this chain into a single state-backed ledger. The Bank of England's Real-Time Gross Settlement renewal, the ECB's TARGET Instant Payment Settlement (TIPS), and cross-border pilots such as Project Dunbar (BIS, 2022) all explore this direction. But efficiency is not an unqualified good. Faster settlement means faster contagion during crisis; reduced intermediation means reduced friction, but also reduced buffers. The elimination of delay is the elimination of pause—useful for commerce, perilous for panic.

The third rationale—monetary transmission—is more subtle and more political. Central banks wield influence through interest rates and reserve requirements, but their effects diffuse through a web of intermediaries. A retail CBDC could offer a direct lever: stimulus deposited instantly into citizens' wallets, or, in more extreme scenarios, negative interest rates applied automatically to idle balances. Such instruments make policy transmission surgical. They also make it personal. A society that accepts programmable stimulus must also accept programmable penalty. The same mechanism that can deliver relief can enforce austerity. This duality is the silent hinge of the CBDC debate: precision policymaking is indistinguishable, in form, from precision control.

A credible counter-argument holds that these dangers can be contained through design and governance. Privacy-preserving architectures such as zero-knowledge proofs can enable compliance without surveillance; tiered systems can protect small transactions while monitoring large ones; intermediated models can shield citizens from direct state oversight. The European Central Bank's prototype digital euro integrates such layers, limiting the information accessible to the central bank itself. But privacy by architecture must contend with politics by appetite. Once programmability exists, incentives to use it will grow—first for convenience, then for policy, then for security. The boundary between optional and mandatory will blur not through conspiracy, but through bureaucracy.

The comparison with crypto assets clarifies what CBDCs *aren't*. Bitcoin's core innovation was to replace institutional trust with algorithmic consensus, enabling settlement without an issuer. A CBDC does the opposite: it anchors settlement in the issuer itself. The two systems share a fascination with transparency and immutability, but their governance is inverted. Bitcoin's trustlessness is adversarial; CBDCs' trust is hierarchical. Both are experiments in credible rules, but one enforces them through open computation, the other through institutional authority. The irony is that, in responding to the challenge of crypto, central banks are adopting some of its tools while rejecting its premise. The state is learning to speak in code, but only to preserve its monopoly on money.

The tension between innovation and incumbency defines this moment. The People's Bank of China's progress has galvanised peers from the European Central Bank to the Federal Reserve, each accelerating feasibility studies lest sovereignty be ceded to foreign rails or private stablecoins. Yet haste carries risk. A CBDC rushed to market without clear boundaries could disintermediate banks, unsettle credit creation, and politicise payments. A system meant to safeguard public trust could erode it. The choice is not between issuing or abstaining, but between designing money as infrastructure or as instrument.

The motif that threads these questions is simple: *public money reborn.* The CBDC revives the state's direct relationship with its citizens, not through cash in hand but through code on a ledger. Whether that rebirth becomes renewal or regression will depend less on algorithms than on accountability. The more programmable money becomes, the more constitutional its design must be. Central bankers once concerned with inflation targets and balance sheets now find themselves arbiters of digital rights.

As pilots expand—from China's e-CNY to the European Union's digital euro, from Nigeria's eNaira to the Bahamas' Sand Dollar—the practical experiments will multiply. Yet the conceptual test remains singular. Can the state issue programmable money without programming behaviour? Can it deliver efficiency and inclusion without eroding privacy and competition? A CBDC that passes those tests would mark progress. One that fails them would mark the quiet end of monetary freedom dressed as reform. The ledger will record both outcomes; history will decide which balance prevails.

Programmability and the Fine Print of Freedom

In December 2020, residents of Suzhou opened their phones to find digital "red packets" of China's e-CNY credited to their wallets. The vouchers, issued by the People's Bank of China through local banks, arrived with two quiet conditions: they expired within days and could be spent only at participating merchants. No cash flew. No notes changed hands. A line of code enforced both rules. The public learned a simple lesson at scale: when money becomes software, money inherits software's clauses. The clause lives in code.

Programmability promises speed, precision, and reach. It also smuggles policy into payment. To understand what that means, we must separate three powers often conflated in debate: *who writes the conditions*, *who audits their use*, and *who may refuse them*. Each power can deliver care—targeted aid, safer rails—or control—behavioural nudges, blacklists, and penalties dressed as "efficiency". The motif that will guide this subchapter is the *fine print*: not the headline that announces a new digital currency, but the buried line that decides whether a citizen spends freely, waits, or asks permission.

Show → Name → Explain → Implication. Start with automated compliance, the seemingly innocuous feature that allows transactions to check themselves against rules before they clear. Name the practice: real-time screening against sanction lists, merchant category codes, spending caps, and identity tokens. Explain the mechanism: a CBDC ledger, or the wallets attached to it, can embed logic that rejects, flags, or routes transactions based on policy. Implication: where banks once enforced rules ex post, code enforces them ex ante. The tug from audit to algorithm is not merely faster compliance; it is a change in constitutional posture. The presumption of permission flips.

The Suzhou pilot showed the benign face of such logic—expiry and merchant scopes intended to stimulate local commerce. Nigeria's eNaira launch in October 2021 illustrated a different edge: despite government backing, adoption faltered because trust and utility were thin. People preferred established mobile-money channels run by private providers. The behaviour was observable: merchants declined eNaira where acceptance tools lagged; citizens kept balances elsewhere; the central bank responded with incentives and outreach. High programmability could not conjure demand. The implication is sobering. If the fine print does not match lived needs, code is just code.

Now widen the aperture. Negative interest rates have sat on European balance sheets since mid-2014; central banks implemented them indirectly through deposits and tiering. A retail CBDC could make the same instrument surgical. Name the policy lever: a time-varying rate on wallet balances above a threshold, applied automatically each day. Explain the machinery: the ledger computes; no bank intermediation is required; exemptions can be parameterised by age, income, or geography. Implication: a macroeconomic tool becomes a personal thermostat. Its merit—clean transmission—arrives tied to its danger—undeniable reach. A society that applauds programmable stimulus must squarely face programmable penalty.

Conditional transfers sit at the centre of that trade-off. During the pandemic, finance ministries worldwide searched for faster ways to deliver cash while ensuring it met urgent goals—food, rent, medicine. A CBDC that encodes "where", "when", and "for what" could cut waste and speed relief. It could also embed paternalism. Who drafts the eligible categories? Who revises them? Who handles wrongful denials? If a citizen's aid cannot buy fuel because a policy engine mislabels a station, where is the counter? The questions are not abstractions. They are help-desk tickets waiting to exist.

Two named, checkable examples sharpen the frame. First, the Bahamas' Sand Dollar, launched nationwide in October 2020, emphasised resilience and inclusion in a hurricane-prone archipelago. Offline features and partnerships with local institutions aimed to keep payments functioning when cards and ATMs fail. The behaviour is measured in drills and outages: whether point-of-sale terminals settle once connectivity returns; whether small merchants actually prefer Sand Dollar to cash when the grid blinks. The fine print here protects freedom by promising continuity. Second, the European Central Bank's digital euro prototypes (2022–2023) explored *tiered privacy*, with "offline small payments" shielded from central visibility and higher-value transfers subject to standard checks. Again the behaviour is the point: whether a citizen can buy a newspaper without creating a record, whether a journalist can pay a source without a file, and whether controls escalate transparently when thresholds are crossed. The clause lives in code—and in credible limits.

A credible counter-example argues that programmability can be ring-fenced. Projects under the Bank for International Settlements—Rosalind (Bank of England/BIS, 2023) and Aurum (HKMA/BIS, 2022)—have demonstrated ways to separate the *instrument* from the *condition engines*, using APIs to keep the core ledger simple while allowing private-sector logic at the edges. In this view, the state issues plain digital cash; intermediaries innovate services; competition and standards discipline excess. The reconciliation is practical rather than theological. Edge programmability is safer than base-layer paternalism, but only if three safeguards hold: public standards define what may be checked; audits verify that private engines do only that; and exit remains real for users who prefer unconditioned rails for lawful activity. Without those, "edge" becomes euphemism for "elsewhere, unaccountable".

Pair abstractions with behaviours. *Trust* is not a white paper; it is the ability to contest a wrongful flag and win. *Efficiency* is not an aggregate metric; it is the number of taps until a parent buys school shoes. *Risk* is not a footnote; it is the morning a pensioner finds her wallet locked because her ID token expired and the help line is busy. Design that does not surface those moments is not neutral; it is negligent.

The fine print also governs *who may refuse*. An opt-out that lives only in a press release is not an opt-out. A real one has three parts: a legal right to hold and use physical cash or digital equivalent without penalty; a practical path to acquire and spend it where people actually live and trade; and a technical mode—*offline small payments*—with a privacy floor enforced in hardware, not adjustable by a patch. If any link is missing, choice devolves to rhetoric. Here, Sweden's e-krona pilots and the ECB's "offline" explorations offer useful prototypes: load a capped amount to a secure element; transact privately within limits; reconcile later; keep the central bank blind by design. It is not perfect privacy. It is privacy with teeth.

Geopolitics now intrudes. The sanctioning of certain crypto mixers in August 2022, and the subsequent choice by some Ethereum relays to filter interactions, revealed how quickly policy can shape programmable money even outside state systems. For CBDCs, the stakes are higher. A country that embeds blacklists at the base layer inherits the power—and the responsibility—to adjudicate identity disputes at the speed of retail payments. Errors propagate instantly; appeals will not. The safe pattern is to keep base-layer validity indifferent to identity and enforce compliance at issuance, redemption, and conversion points. The dangerous pattern is to confuse *who may hold* with *what is valid.* The first is policy. The second is physics.

Who writes the conditions? The obvious answer—parliament or central bank—will not suffice. In practice, the "rule writers" will be a web of agencies, standards bodies, and private providers, from tax authorities to AML regulators to wallet developers and point-of-sale vendors. Each will want a hook. Each hook becomes a clause. Without a constitutional framework that limits hooks in number and scope, programmability becomes accretion. The bill grows until users cannot pay without passing through four checks, three logs, two consents, and one paternal veto. This is not dystopia. It is bureaucracy winning.

Who audits the writers? Two layers matter. First, code audits—independent verification that the engines do only what the law permits and log only what the law allows. Second, *policy audits*—regular, published reviews of the rulebook itself, with quantified measures of false positives, dispute outcomes, and time-to-restore access for wrongly blocked users. A central bank that can report "average time to unlock after wrongful freeze: 2 hours; 95th percentile: 24 hours; appeals upheld: 37%" treats freedom as a service level, not a slogan. Numbers discipline power.

Who may refuse? True refusal is exit without penalty. A business that accepts only conditioned money narrows citizens' choices as effectively as a law. A state that waives fees and identity checks for *very small* payments in public spaces keeps genuine anonymity alive. A transport network that accepts *offline small payments* on buses and trains preserves privacy where it matters. The social signal travels both ways. If citizens observe that the only place unconditioned money still works is a museum gift shop, they will learn what they need to know.

Two more examples, mechanical and measurable, make the stakes concrete. First, *expiry*. The Suzhou vouchers were modest and experimental. Now imagine budget-cycle "use-by" dates on public salaries, or seasonal spending windows tied to macro targets. The code is trivial. The politics is not. Expiry can help in crisis; it also creates a habit. The stress test is simple: what would it take to prohibit expiry by default and require a supermajority, with a sunset, to deploy it even in emergencies? If the answer is "an internal policy memo", the fine print is already writing citizens out of their own wallets. Second, *category locks*. Merchant category codes (MCCs) are old tools; using them to constrain everyday CBDC spending would be new. The drill here is to publish the list, the process to change it, and the appeal route when misclassification blocks a lawful purchase. A democracy that hides its category list is not hiding a secret. It is hiding a habit.

A credible limitation shadows every call for restraint: crime and corruption are real. Fully anonymous rails at scale invite abuse. The reconciliation is design, not denial. Set hard floors for private, offline small payments. Set hard caps for cumulative private usage per period. Make larger transactions conditional, visible, and disputable. Build the audit layer outside the central bank; publish statistics that show enforcement without voyeurism. One can price privacy without abolishing it. A currency is not safer because no one can pass unnoticed; it is safer because bad actors are found without turning everyone else into a suspect.

Return to the motif. The fine print decides whether a CBDC is care or control. It lives in code, policy, and defaults. Defaults matter most. A wallet that toggles "privacy mode" on by default for small payments sends a different message than one that buries it behind three menus and a warning. A help line that restores access quickly, without humiliating questions, signals that the state understands trust as a practice. A public commitment to *no expiry by default* and *no category blocks by default*, backed by statutory teeth, does more to legitimate a CBDC than any white paper.

The unresolved test is simple, and it cannot be delegated to engineers. How much conditionality will a society accept in the name of care, and how much discretion will it tolerate in the name of control? The next policy cycle will offer easy temptations—targeted relief, green rebates, fraud clamps—each one a clause away. The question is whether legislators will write a constitution for programmable money before the clauses accrete, and whether citizens will notice while they can still refuse. The clause lives in code. Who holds the pen?

Architecture Choices: Retail, Wholesale, and Intermediated

On 20 October 2020 in Nassau, the Central Bank of The Bahamas switched on the Sand Dollar nationwide. Cards and mobile wallets began settling payments even when storms cut power to the out islands; small shops recorded sales that would once have waited for a working terminal. The system delivered something concrete: resilience in a hurricane belt. It also delivered a signal. Architecture is policy. The Sand Dollar's retail design—central bank money in citizens' phones, distributed through private intermediaries—traded some privacy for continuity, some bank primacy for public access. The decision was not about apps. It was about balance. Design chooses winners.

"Retail", "wholesale", and "intermediated" are labels for how that balance is struck. Each choice rewires three constitutive elements—who holds the claim, how settlement completes, and what data the state can see—and through them reshapes privacy, resilience, and the banking structure that sits atop the state's balance sheet. The motif that will guide this subchapter is a simple one: *who holds the keys?* Not metaphorically; literally. In a retail CBDC, citizens or their wallet providers hold spending keys to a public liability. In a wholesale

CBDC, banks hold keys to a rail that modernises settlement pipes. In an intermediated design, keys and customer-touch sit with private providers while final settlement and rule enforcement sit with the central bank. These keys unlock different futures.

Show → Name → Explain → Implication. Start with retail. Show: a parent in Freeport paying for groceries offline during an outage; a merchant reconciling later when the network returns; balances held as claims on the central bank itself. Name: the Sand Dollar. Explain: the architecture gives households direct access to public money via regulated wallet providers who perform KYC/AML and provide user interfaces, while the central bank maintains a core ledger and rules. Implication: resilience rises—no single card processor stands between buyer and seller—but so does the central bank's proximity to households. Privacy must be engineered, not assumed. Bank funding models must be protected with caps or remuneration to prevent deposit flight during stress.

Wholesale tells a different story. Show: in Singapore and Canada between 2016 and 2019, MAS and the Bank of Canada ran Projects Ubin and Jasper, settling interbank obligations with tokenised central bank money; in Switzerland, Project Helvetia linked the SNB and SIX to settle tokenised securities DvP on real infrastructure. Name: wholesale CBDC pilots. Explain: these designs restrict access to banks and FMIs, preserving the two-tier system while giving it new rails—atomic DvP, extended operating hours, and cross-ledger interoperability. Implication: privacy is easier (participants are regulated institutions), resilience improves in the plumbing, and bank structure is largely untouched. Wholesale CBDC is a plumbing upgrade with constitutional consequences only at the edges.

Intermediated retail sits between these poles. Show: the European Central Bank's digital euro preparatory work from 2020 to 2023, where private payment service providers would run wallets, onboard users, and handle day-to-day interactions, while the Eurosystem would operate the settlement core and define standards for privacy and offline use. Name: an intermediated retail architecture. Explain: the model seeks to deliver public money to citizens without putting the central bank in the business of consumer service or competition with banks, using tiered privacy (e.g., *offline small payments* with hardware-based anonymity and higher-value payments with standard checks) and *holding limits* or tiered remuneration to reduce bank disintermediation risk. Implication: much depends on defaults. If intermediaries over-collect data, privacy fails in practice; if holding limits are too tight, utility suffers; if they are too loose, deposits shift. Intermediation is not a compromise; it is an allocation of power.

Privacy changes with each choice because data location changes. Retail direct—citizens banking at the central bank—creates the sharpest tension: the institution that sets policy would see the flow of retail life unless the system is blind by design. The Swedish e-krona pilots responded with *offline small payments* using secure elements to keep tiny transactions unobservable to the issuer. The ECB's prototypes explored "anonymity vouchers" and tiered thresholds. Wholesale is simpler: regulated banks accept institutional transparency and audit. Intermediated retail is the proving ground: the central bank need not see personal data, but PSPs will, unless law and architecture prevent it. The real question is behavioural: does a traveller buy a newspaper anonymously, and does a journalist pay a source without creating a dossier? If not, the label "privacy-preserving" is marketing, not remedy.

Resilience is the next axis. Retail designs can harden payments against outages through *store-and-forward* and offline limits. The Bahamas chose this for reasons written by weather. Nigeria's eNaira, launched in October 2021, emphasised speed and cost but struggled with adoption because resilience in human terms—merchant acceptance, reliable connectivity, trusted support—lagged. Wholesale CBDC raises resilience where markets notice least: synchronised settlement between platforms, extended hours, and less dependency on correspondent chains. Intermediated systems must prove both: that they can operate when a major PSP goes down and that the core can continue without a dominant vendor. The metrics are not white-paper glossaries but drills: time to recover from a PSP outage; percentage of transactions that settle offline successfully within reconciliation windows; proportion of critical infrastructure that can operate when the cross-border link fails.

Bank structure is the third axis, and here retail CBDC is a live wire. If households substitute deposits for central bank money—

especially in panic—banks lose a cheap, stable funding base. Lending contracts or must be replaced by wholesale funding at worse terms. This is the *disintermediation risk*. Design tools exist. Caps per user limit flight during stress; tiered remuneration makes large CBDC balances unattractive; mandated pass-through funding windows allow banks to borrow central bank money secured by CBDC inflows. The ECB, Bank of England, and BIS have discussed each in turn. But tools are not neutral. Caps reduce the instrument's usefulness; negative remuneration invites political heat; special funding windows add a new umbilical cord between banks and the state. Wholesale CBDC dodges this by staying off the retail beach. Intermediated retail walks it with care.

Two named, checkable examples anchor these trade-offs. First, Project mBridge, the BIS Innovation Hub collaboration with the central banks of Hong Kong, Thailand, the UAE, and China's PBOC, has tested a shared cross-border wholesale CBDC platform. Show: banks in different jurisdictions settling with each other on a common ledger, with atomic PvP reducing settlement risk and time. Explain: sovereignty is preserved at the currency layer while interoperability is achieved at the platform layer. Implication: wholesale architecture can shift geopolitics in the pipes—reducing dependence on legacy correspondent networks—without touching retail privacy directly. Second, the ECB's digital euro path. Show: an intermediated retail design with "offline" and "online" modes, PSPs at the edge, and central bank control of standards. Explain: this attempts to square inclusion, resilience, and bank stability with legal constraints on data. Implication: its success will be judged not by press releases but by defaults—how much the central bank truly cannot see and whether banks still fund lending on terms that keep credit flowing.

A credible counter-example warns against architectural overreach. Nigeria's eNaira, despite being a retail CBDC, saw sluggish take-up through 2022–2023. The design promised low-cost payments, but merchants resisted where integration was thin and citizens stuck with mobile money rails they trusted. The reconciliation is blunt. Architecture cannot manufacture adoption. It can only remove friction and uphold rights. If the wallet is clumsy, the help line slow, and the merchant terminal missing, no liability structure will save the system. Conversely, when architecture meets a lived need, as in the Bahamas' offline features or the ECB's proposed *offline small payments*, utility speaks for itself.

This brings us to the *decision matrix*—not a chart on a slide, but a set of questions that reveal priorities by forcing measurement.

Who holds the keys, and where are they stored? If citizens hold keys in secure elements for small amounts, privacy has a floor. If keys live in cloud wallets controlled by PSPs, privacy depends on contract. If the central bank can rotate keys centrally, resilience to loss rises and personal autonomy falls. Choose.

What can the issuer see by default? If the answer is "aggregate flows and compliance flags", the system has a chance to feel like cash. If the answer is "transaction-level data with legal promises of restraint", politics will eventually test those promises. Design for blindness, not benevolence.

How does settlement behave under stress? Measure peak transaction-per-second during drills; measure reconciliation errors after offline bursts; measure failover times between PSPs and the core. A retail system that collapses during a regional blackout or cyber event is an elegant toy. A wholesale system that cannot coordinate with tokenised asset platforms will be bypassed by private rails.

What happens to bank funding during a scare? Model deposit outflows with realistic caps and tiered rates; publish the standing facilities that will backfill funding; commit to the cadence at which those facilities can expand. If the plan is "trust us", the plan is blank.

What is the cross-border story? Wholesale CBDC can stitch corridors where politics permits; intermediated retail can interoperate through standards and FX venues; direct retail cross-border CBDCs raise sovereignty questions immediately. Decide whether your priority is sanctions enforcement, remittance cost, or interoperability with allies, and tune the interface accordingly.

A further hinge in any matrix is governance. Who can change parameters—caps, rates, offline limits—and how quickly? The temptation to manage behaviour by patch is real. A constitution for the currency should pre-commit: changing offline caps requires parliamentary approval; adding merchant category blocks requires a supermajority and sunsets; activating negative remuneration triggers automatic reporting on distributional effects. The behaviour to seek is boring: a change log with legal citations and review windows, not a blog post.

None of these choices are free of risk. Retail CBDC maximises inclusion potential and policy transmission but threatens deposit stability and privacy through proximity. Wholesale CBDC modernises critical plumbing, improves cross-border efficiency, and leaves households alone, but does little for retail costs or access in the near term. Intermediated retail spreads responsibility and uses existing distribution but can recreate surveillance in private hands and entrench incumbents. Trade-offs are not solved; they are priced.

Return to the motif. *Who holds the keys?* In a retail system that honours liberal norms, citizens hold small-value keys locally and privately; providers hold custodial keys with liability and audit; the central bank holds rule-keys, not spending keys. In wholesale, banks hold keys and meet heightened operational duties; the central bank holds the ultimate consensus-key for settlement. In an intermediated model, the keyring is shared: the central bank enforces the constitution; PSPs face the public; citizens retain a domain of no-questions-asked offline spend. If that domain shrinks in practice, the architecture has answered the wrong question.

The forward test is clear and uncomfortable. Under stress—from a bank wobble, a cyber incident, or a political crisis—which promises break first: caps meant to protect banks, privacy meant to protect citizens, or interoperability meant to protect commerce? Design that expects stress will specify the order in which constraints loosen and who must authorise each step. Design that does not will improvise—and improvise away the very freedoms it proclaimed. The architecture is a decision. Who holds the keys when the siren sounds?

Geopolitics of Rails

On 26 February 2022 in Brussels, the European Commission announced that selected Russian banks would be cut off from SWIFT. Within hours, compliance teams in Frankfurt, London, and New York reconfigured filters; correspondent banks paused transfers; trade finance froze. Oil still flowed and contracts still stood, yet a handful of messages no longer routed. The result was immediate: payments failed not because money had vanished, but because the rail had. Rails move power, not promises. A sanction became a software change, and a foreign-policy tool proved to be a payments switch.

That moment laid bare an old truth with new machinery: settlement networks are instruments of statecraft. In the twentieth century, this meant clearing houses, reserve accounts, and maritime choke points. In the twenty-first, it means API gates, node lists, and protocol rules. Central Bank Digital Currencies (CBDCs) push this logic further. If public money becomes programmable and interoperable across borders, the rail itself can encode policy. The choice is stark and technical: design rails to reinforce sanctions and alliances—or design them to route around them. Either way, geopolitics is written in code.

Show → Name → Explain → Implication. Start with the clearest show. The SWIFT exclusions—confirmed by the Council of the EU in late February 2022—demonstrated how messaging standards and shared directories act as levers. Name the actors: SWIFT in La Hulpe; national central banks; the U.S. Treasury's OFAC; the European Commission. Explain the mechanism: when a bank's BIC is suspended and counterparty banks update filters, international transfers stall even if balances still exist in nostro accounts. Implication: interoperability itself is a policy weapon. A network that most banks must use becomes a single point of sanction.

CBDCs change the theatre but not the play. Wholesale projects like the BIS Innovation Hub's mBridge—tested in 2022–2023 with the Hong Kong Monetary Authority, the Bank of Thailand, the Central Bank of the UAE, and the People's Bank of China—show how multiple central banks can share a common ledger to settle cross-border payments instantly, with atomic delivery-versus-payment across currencies. Name it: mBridge. Explain the mechanism: each participant issues wholesale CBDC on a shared platform; commercial banks access corridors to trade and settle under rules agreed by the central banks. Implication: the coalition that controls the corridor controls the policy embedded in it—eligibility, data visibility, and dispute resolution. The rail becomes a club with code as its charter.

A second example, quieter and just as instructive, sits in China's Cross-Border Interbank Payment System (CIPS), which predates CBDCs but foreshadows them. CIPS clears and settles renminbi transactions, often in coordination with SWIFT messaging. Its growth has been steady; its governance is domestic; its purpose is strategic. Explain the mechanism: by offering a sovereign alternative to correspondent banking chains dominated by dollar rails, China reduces exposure to Western policy levers. Implication: when CBDC corridors arrive, they will not appear ex nihilo. They will grow from these national systems, inheriting their politics.

The counter-example is as important as the thesis. Interoperability is hard. Cross-border payments require not only messaging but identity assurance, anti–money laundering coordination, and foreign-exchange liquidity under volatile conditions. Project Icebreaker—run by the BIS with the central banks of Israel, Norway, and Sweden in 2023—demonstrated a model where domestic CBDC systems connect through a hub that handles FX bids. It worked in pilots. But scaling such models means aligning privacy laws, audit rights, and recourse procedures across jurisdictions that distrust one another. The reconciliation is sober: CBDCs can change the hardware of settlement, but the software of geopolitics—treaties, norms, and leverage—still gates outcomes. Rails lower friction; they do not dissolve strategy.

To see how CBDCs can reinforce sanctions, consider how programmability and membership lists intersect. A wholesale rail can embed rule engines that enforce blacklists at proposal time, not merely at reconciliation. Show the behaviour: a bank attempts to settle a payment to a sanctioned entity; the platform's smart contract rejects the transaction before it broadcasts to peers. Name the policy:

pre-trade compliance baked into settlement logic. Explain: by moving checks from edge systems into the core ledger, false negatives fall and policy bite rises. Implication: sanction enforcement becomes an algorithm with audit trails. The upside is clarity; the downside is centralisation of discretionary power.

To see how CBDCs can resist sanctions, change the coalition. A corridor built by states outside the dominant sanctioning blocs can define screening rules differently, lower data disclosure, or insist on bilateral, not multilateral, oversight of settlement. Show: a commodity invoice is financed through a corridor that clears in digital dirhams and digital yuan; screening focuses on terrorist finance and fraud, not on Western foreign-policy priorities. Explain: the rail enforces the policy of its members. Implication: the more credible and liquid such corridors become, the weaker the bite of sanctions applied through legacy rails alone. The lever survives; its leverage shrinks.

The motif that will thread through this subchapter is the *switch*. Who holds it, where it sits, and which lights it controls. In mBridge-like infrastructures, the switch is a shared governance module with voting thresholds and emergency powers. In domestic CBDCs, the switch is the rulebook that wallets must implement to access the base layer. At the retail edge, the switch becomes granular: a "travel rule" that follows a payment across borders, a compliance oracle that flags risky destinations, an offline mode that narrows in hostile jurisdictions. Every switch location reveals who can darken a corridor and at what cost.

Pair abstractions with behaviours. *Trust* is not a slogan; it is a bank's decision to commit liquidity to a corridor every morning. *Efficiency* is not a brochure; it is the measured time from payment instruction to finality across currencies, net of FX slippage. *Risk* is not a footnote; it is the share of a country's trade invoiced in a rail it does not control, multiplied by the number of policy disputes it expects in a decade. These are computable questions. Ministries already compute them.

CBDCs also rearrange surveillance. In legacy correspondent banking, data scatter across banks, messaging providers, and regulators. In a CBDC corridor, data can centralise in platform logs by design. The benefit is investigatory speed; the hazard is geopolitical voyeurism. Who can query what, and how fast? Is there a joint audit court with both technical and diplomatic standing? Without such institutions, the temptation will be strong for the largest member to treat the corridor as a panopticon. The switch dims, and trust follows.

Consider two further named episodes that illuminate the stakes. First, the U.S. Treasury's designations against certain crypto mixers in August 2022 cascaded into Ethereum's relay layer as some builders and relays filtered interactions to avoid downstream legal risk. That was not a CBDC event. It was a rehearsal. It showed how quickly policy can reach into programmable rails when intermediaries concentrate. If a similar concentration emerges in CBDC corridors—say, one dominant relay or gateway—policy will ride the chokepoint. Second, Russia's SPFS, its domestic alternative to SWIFT, reportedly expanded connections after 2022, while bilateral invoicing in non-dollar currencies rose in some trade flows. The effect was partial, not total. It shows both the ceiling and the direction: fragmentation raises costs, but it also builds resilience to specific levers.

Sovereignty is the throughline. A state that depends entirely on foreign-owned message buses and settlement platforms carries a latent veto in its economy. CBDCs offer a way to domesticate that risk or share it among allies. Yet sovereignty without liquidity is theatre. A rail that cannot clear oil, wheat, chips, and debt at scale will stay decorative. The practical question for any finance ministry is dull and decisive: what share of critical imports and exports can settle, at tolerable spreads, on rails we can keep alive during a crisis? If the answer is small, strategy must start with trade structure, not wallet apps.

The decision matrix that emerges is not ideological; it is architectural. Which partners share our screening standards? Which currencies provide deep FX books against ours? Which legal systems can bind disputes across the platform? Which identity schemes can map to each other without erasing privacy? Which audit regimes can verify compliance without giving a rival state live visibility into our economy? Each "which" is a build-or-ally choice. Build alone and gain control, lose scale; build with allies and gain scale, share control.

There is, inevitably, a cost to multiplying rails. Fragmentation creates incompatibilities; bridges import risk; liquidity splinters. The private sector will arbitrage differences, routing flows through the cheapest and least intrusive corridors. That is both a feature and a vulnerability. In crisis, corporates will race to whichever rail still clears. In peace, they will pressure regulators to allow access to rails beyond the state's preferred alliance map. The switch will be contested in boardrooms as well as cabinets.

CBDCs also invite quiet forms of coercion short of sanctions. A platform's governance can set subtle defaults: settlement windows that favour some time zones, technical standards that privilege some identity schemes, fee structures that burden small counterparties, limits that slow capital exit without naming it. Each default is a diplomatic instrument. In the past, the dollar's network effects made many defaults American by inertia. In the future, multiple CBDC corridors may make defaults geopolitical by negotiation. Whoever writes the default wins a little without a fight.

A credible limitation tempers triumphalism. Many sanctioned actors already use informal value transfer systems, commodity barter, or third-country intermediaries to evade restrictions. CBDCs do not abolish that shadow. Indeed, if public rails become more surveilled, shadows may deepen for those intent on abuse. The reconciliation is honest. CBDCs can tighten compliance where compliance is already a norm; they cannot make pariahs behave. The strategic value lies in making evasion expensive and alliance signalling clear.

Return to the motif. The switch sits in several hands. Domestic parliaments set constitutional limits for their CBDCs—privacy floors, offline caps, access rights. Central banks and treasuries negotiate corridor rules—membership, screening, data access. Firms decide day by day whether to place orders through one rail or another. Citizens experience the outcome as a payment that clears—or fails—with a message that names a policy rather than a balance. The switch must be governed as a public utility, even when it spans borders.

So the forward test is this: can a coalition design a cross-border CBDC rail that enforces its shared policies without becoming a single point of diplomatic failure? Can it publish rulebooks, audit logs, and redress mechanisms robust enough that firms commit liquidity voluntarily? Can it, when sanctions are necessary, demonstrate that refusals are specific, lawful, and reversible—so that the rail remains attractive after the crisis? Or will the world split into mirrored corridors, each efficient inside, antagonistic outside, and brittle at the seams?

The answer will not be voted once. It will be measured—by how much trade settles where; by how quickly crises propagate along some rails and dampen along others; by how often the switch is pulled, and with what justification. Payment networks have become foreign-policy tools. The code is being written now. Who writes it, and who can rewrite it, is the strategic question of monetary statecraft in the programmable age.

Chapter 5
Stablecoins — Dollar Hegemony by Other Means

On 11 May 2022, a South Korean stablecoin named TerraUSD lost its peg to the U.S. dollar. Within 48 hours, forty billion dollars in notional value evaporated; within a week, retail investors were posting screenshots of balances that had fallen to pennies. The peg that was supposed to be algorithmic turned out to be psychological. A feedback loop of fear, redemptions, and collapsing collateral unstitched a monetary fiction that had held for months. The crash was not only a technical failure. It was a rehearsal for a deeper question: what does it mean when the dollar's dominance is rebuilt not through central banks, but through code?

Stablecoins promise digital stability in a volatile financial universe, yet their architecture reveals how fragile "stability" can be when trust migrates from institutions to mechanisms. The paradox is stark. These tokens exist to escape banks—and yet depend utterly on banking infrastructure. They market decentralisation—but rest on dollar reserves held in custodial accounts. They seek to globalise access—but encode one currency's supremacy in every line of their protocol. The dollar, far from being dethroned, is quietly reasserting itself as the substrate of the digital age.

At their core, stablecoins are attempts to recreate three functions of money—store of value, medium of exchange, and unit of account—without the sovereign guarantees that anchor traditional currencies. Each project chooses a trinity of trade-offs: *collateral*, *convertibility*, and *credibility*. Some, like Tether (USDT) or USD Coin (USDC), anchor to fiat reserves, offering one-to-one redemption promises backed by short-term Treasuries or cash equivalents. Others, like Dai, mix crypto collateral with governance algorithms. Still others, like TerraUSD before its collapse, relied on a balancing act of code and confidence. Each model works—until the day it doesn't. And that day usually arrives when markets go quiet, not when they scream. Fragility hides best in calm.

Collateral defines the boundary between promise and panic. Convertibility is the daily ritual that tests that boundary. Credibility is the sum of both—until it isn't. In tranquil periods, stablecoins clear billions in remittances and trading liquidity, lubricating decentralised finance and offshore commerce. But when redemption lines grow long or reserves opaque, confidence becomes a race condition. The dollar's credibility, borrowed through exposure to U.S. Treasuries, sustains the system. Yet that dependency also extends Washington's reach: stablecoins may live on blockchains, but their heartbeats sync to the U.S. money market.

Why, then, do the peripheries adopt first? The answer is less ideological than it is practical. In Argentina, Nigeria, Turkey, and Venezuela, ordinary savers turn to dollar-linked tokens not because they admire crypto's ethos, but because their local currencies cannot hold value across a month. Stablecoins are used for salaries, cross-border freelancing, and remittances. Tether's daily volumes in emerging markets often exceed those of national banks. Demand maps to pain, not persuasion. Marketing cannot counterfeit necessity. The first adopters are not technologists chasing yield, but families escaping inflation—one dollar proxy at a time.

In remittance corridors, stablecoins turn smartphones into offshore accounts. Workers in São Paulo or Manila can send value in seconds to relatives in rural areas who would otherwise face days of delay and layers of fees. Yet these same tokens, when scaled, create parallel monetary systems where the local central bank's power to influence credit and liquidity weakens. The logic repeats an old imperial pattern: the periphery dollarises itself while the core debates theory. Stablecoins are the new dollarisation, written in Solidity instead of policy memos.

Regulation, when it finally arrives, will decide whether stablecoins institutionalise or ossify. Licensing and reserve rules can function as both moat and muzzle. A licence grants legitimacy, inviting institutional money and reassuring users. It also raises barriers, favouring incumbents who can absorb compliance costs and integrate with banks. Regulation transforms market experiments into semi-public infrastructure—and, in doing so, domesticates their revolutionary edge. When U.S. authorities pressed issuers to disclose holdings and hold Treasury bills rather than commercial paper, stability improved but decentralisation evaporated. Safety trades against openness, every time.

The political dimension is sharper still. If a stablecoin is redeemable only through U.S.-regulated banks, then its global reach is ultimately conditional on U.S. policy. Should a future administration extend sanctions or compliance lists into on-chain ecosystems, the same rails that empower global access could enforce geopolitical exclusion. The dollar, embedded inside the protocol, carries its foreign policy with it. Each token is a soft ambassador of U.S. monetary power, travelling faster and farther than the Federal Reserve ever could.

Yet the story is not simply imperial continuity. It is also the tale of creative adaptation at the edges of the system. The Philippines' blockchain remittance firms, Kenya's mobile-money hybrids, and Latin America's dollar-linked savings apps each show how necessity breeds experimentation. When the official financial system cannot deliver predictable value, people improvise. Stablecoins provide the duct tape of digital commerce: messy, effective, and increasingly indispensable. That very usefulness makes them hard to outlaw and harder to ignore.

Their endurance will depend on how they weather stress. Redemption mechanics, liquidity buffers, and transparency audits will determine whether these instruments survive a global liquidity crunch or implode under their own opacity. The test will come not from innovation's peaks but from its troughs—when risk-free rates spike, when counterparties default, when redemptions outrun cash flow. In those moments, credibility gaps will open like sinkholes. The question will not be whether code is sound, but whether confidence is justified.

The motif threading through this chapter is the *mirror*. Every stablecoin reflects the system it claims to replace. Its collateral sits in the same instruments that anchor the fiat world; its users seek the same stability that national currencies promise; its failures echo the same panics that history has rehearsed. The mirror flatters no one.

It reveals that even the most decentralised architecture cannot escape the gravitational pull of the dollar.

What follows in this chapter is an examination of that paradox in full: the mechanics that hold the peg, the incentives that drive adoption, the regulatory choices that shape legitimacy, and the geopolitical logic that turns digital tokens into instruments of soft power. Behind every line of code lies an old question—who issues, who redeems, and who decides what is safe? Stablecoins were supposed to unbundle money from the state; instead, they may be scripting the next chapter of its dominion.

The reader should leave this introduction not with reassurance but with curiosity sharpened to a point. If stability is always relative, then so is sovereignty. When a blockchain token promises "one dollar, always", whose dollar is it, and under whose law does that promise hold? The next pages follow that thread—from collateral desks to central banks, from remittance markets to regulatory chambers—tracing how digital dollars could make the old empire invisible, yet omnipresent. The dollar may no longer sit only in vaults or reserves. It now lives inside the protocol.

Collateral, Convertibility, and the Credibility Gap

At 2:38 a.m. on 11 May 2022, traders on Binance and Coinbase watched the price of TerraUSD, an algorithmic stablecoin that promised to hold a steady value of one U.S. dollar, slip below 70 cents. Within hours, redemption queues broke, arbitrage bots jammed mempools, and Luna—the asset meant to stabilise the system—entered a death spiral. Forty billion dollars of notional wealth disappeared within a week. Terraform Labs, once hailed as the architect of a "self-healing" monetary protocol, was later investigated by regulators in Seoul and Washington. The algorithm had worked perfectly in theory, until reality failed to cooperate. The collapse was a parable of misplaced faith: collateral that could not cover claims, convertibility that vanished in crisis, and a credibility gap exposed when confidence was most needed.

The mechanics of stablecoins are as old as banking. For every promise to redeem at par, there must exist sufficient, liquid collateral. Convertibility—the ability to exchange one token for its reference asset at will—is the bridge between code and confidence. The problem, as centuries of monetary history show, is that such bridges always appear strongest in calm weather. From the 1847 railway panics in Britain to the 2008 run on money market funds, tranquil periods breed fragility. Stability itself becomes the most dangerous illusion. The motif that will run through this subchapter is the *mirror test*: every redemption promise forces the system to look at what really backs it—and what only appears to.

Show → Name → Explain → Implication. Begin with the show: Tether Holdings Ltd., issuer of USDT, reported in its March 2024 attestation that over 85% of its $110 billion in reserves were held in short-term U.S. Treasuries, reverse repos, and cash equivalents. Name the entity: Tether, the largest stablecoin issuer by market capitalisation, processing trillions annually across exchanges and offshore corridors. Explain: its model resembles a 19th-century money market fund—dollars in, redeemable tokens out, backed by a portfolio whose safety depends on liquidity under stress. Implication: so long as Treasuries remain liquid and redemption demand is orderly, the peg holds; if yields spike, repo markets jam, or regulatory access falters, the promise is tested in real time.

Contrast this with Circle's USD Coin (USDC), whose reserves—fully segregated and audited by Deloitte—are held in cash and U.S. Treasuries custodied at regulated institutions. When Silicon Valley Bank failed in March 2023, $3.3 billion of Circle's reserves were trapped temporarily in receivership. For thirty-six hours, USDC traded as low as $0.87. Redemption was suspended, not by insolvency, but by logistics. Once the Federal Deposit Insurance Corporation guaranteed deposits, the peg recovered. The show was brief but revealing. Convertibility is not a function of arithmetic; it is a choreography of trust, speed, and access to banking infrastructure. A stablecoin may be solvent yet still illiquid when its counterparties stumble.

Collateral is the backbone of credibility, but the composition of that collateral matters more than headlines suggest. Fully fiat-backed models promise safety through transparency—monthly attestations, auditor signatures, and narrow investment mandates. Crypto-collateralised models, like MakerDAO's Dai, pursue stability through overcollateralisation and algorithmic liquidation. As of mid-2024, over 50% of Dai's collateral consisted of tokenised U.S. Treasury instruments, a quiet admission that decentralised credit eventually loops back to centralised assets. The mechanism works: liquidate risky collateral, mint fewer Dai, stabilise price. Yet it also re-imports the very dependency it sought to escape. The credibility of Dai is therefore conditional not on code alone but on the solvency and liquidity of the U.S. Treasury market itself.

The limitation of algorithmic collateralisation was demonstrated brutally by TerraUSD. Instead of holding reserves, it relied on an arbitrage mechanism: when the stablecoin's price fell, holders could redeem it for a dollar's worth of Luna; when it rose, they could mint new supply. The self-referential loop functioned during optimism but collapsed when demand fell. The Luna collateral shrank faster than it could be created, erasing the redemption path entirely. The implication was structural, not moral: convertibility backed by correlation is not collateral; it is contagion in disguise.

Convertibility itself is a choreography of queues. The promise "one token equals one dollar" is meaningless if the redemption window narrows. Money market funds discovered this during the 2008 crisis when the Reserve Primary Fund "broke the buck" after holding Lehman Brothers paper. Stablecoins mirror that experience daily, but at algorithmic speed. When USDC briefly lost its peg in 2023, exchanges temporarily disabled direct conversions, effectively reintroducing the same gates that money market funds used under stress. The system was saved not by decentralisation but by regulatory backstop. In a sense, the Federal Reserve underwrote the peg indirectly—first through its emergency bank facility, then through restored confidence in insured deposits.

The credibility gap emerges in this junction between perception and structure. Users believe redemption is instant and unconditional; issuers know it is conditional and sequential. The gap widens during stress. It narrows only through either explicit state backing or excess collateral that absorbs shock. Some stablecoin designs, such as

Paxos's USDP, rely on trust in regulated custody and legal redemption rights under New York trust law. Others, like algorithmic experiments, rely on faith in arbitrage incentives. The former codifies dependence on law; the latter on reflexivity. Both are fragile, but in different registers.

Show another concrete example: in August 2020, the decentralised protocol Curve saw its stablecoin pools destabilise when one constituent—sUSD—deviated by just a few cents. Liquidity providers rebalanced aggressively, amplifying volatility across otherwise stable pairs. The metric to watch was slippage, not solvency: even a 1% deviation forced arbitrageurs to drain pools in minutes. Explain: this revealed a systemic truth. In composable financial systems, convertibility is not bilateral but networked; a wobble in one asset propagates across the entire topology. Implication: stress scenarios must model cascades, not silos. Fragility is collective.

The counter-example lies in fiat-backed models under prudential supervision. The Hong Kong Monetary Authority's stablecoin consultation in December 2023 outlined capital and liquidity requirements designed to mimic bank regulation: minimum reserve ratios, redemption within T+1, and independent audits. Such measures anchor credibility through governance rather than code. Yet even here, risks remain. Regulatory legitimacy can confer complacency; participants stop modelling the tail. A token may be safe by law but brittle in implementation if redemption logistics depend on a single custodian or jurisdiction. The reconciliation is pragmatic: true stability requires redundancy—multiple banks, multiple rails, and clear recourse.

The quiet motif of the *mirror test* reappears here. Every issuer faces its reflection during redemption surges. Tether's 2022 stress episode, when it honoured $7 billion in redemptions within 48 hours, demonstrated operational strength. But it also exposed how concentration risk—holding reserves across a narrow set of counterparties—can magnify systemic vulnerability. A similar mirror faced banks in 1907, money market funds in 2008, and crypto lenders in 2022. Each believed their collateral adequate until the crowd asked to see it.

Stress scenarios are therefore less about predicting collapse than rehearsing it. Central banks perform liquidity stress tests precisely because markets forget. For stablecoin issuers, such rehearsals could mean simulated redemption queues, delayed wire tests, and audits of intraday liquidity rather than end-of-month snapshots. The relevant question is behavioural: how fast do users run when doubt starts? Metrics like average holding period, redemption concentration, and inter-exchange transfer latency are leading indicators of panic. Fragility begins not with insolvency but with speed.

Convertibility also intersects with law. When a user redeems, what asset are they legally entitled to? A claim on specific reserves, or a contractual right against an issuer? The distinction defines whether stablecoin holders are creditors or depositors. During the 2023 USDC depeg, Circle's contractual promise to redeem 1:1 in U.S. dollars remained intact; users simply could not access the path. In algorithmic models, no such legal recourse exists—only code paths that can halt, fork, or fail. The implication is profound: credibility cannot be audited solely in balance sheets; it must be underwritten by enforceable rights and tested under stress.

A further paradox appears in the way tranquil periods nurture complacency. When redemptions are rare and secondary markets deep, issuers accumulate risk by stealth. Duration creep—extending maturities to chase yield—quietly erodes liquidity. In early 2022, before the Terra collapse, some stablecoin reserves held commercial paper with 60-day maturities. When panic hit, those assets could not be liquidated without loss. The parallel with money market funds is exact. Stability breeds optimisation; optimisation breeds fragility. The circuit completes when shock arrives.

One credible counter-argument claims that transparency can substitute for redundancy. Publish holdings daily, and markets will self-correct. The evidence is mixed. Tether's move toward quarterly attestations in 2023 improved confidence, yet redemption waves still follow rumours, not reports. Visibility may deter deception but cannot eliminate fear. The mirror reflects what it sees, not what it hides.

The quiet motif returns again: in the mirror, the system must decide what kind of money it wants to be. A narrow instrument redeemable on demand? A mutual fund proxy? A synthetic deposit subject to bank-like rules? Each definition entails a regulatory consequence. If it behaves like a deposit, it invites deposit insurance and supervision. If it behaves like a fund, it inherits disclosure and diversification mandates. Pretending to be neither only delays accountability. Convertibility without classification is theatre.

The forward test is direct and uncomfortable. Could any major stablecoin honour 50% of its outstanding tokens for cash within a week, across multiple jurisdictions, without central bank aid? If not, its peg is conditional, not absolute. The next stress event will not announce itself; it will begin as a routine redemption day that fails to clear. Collateral will matter, but choreography will matter more—the sequencing of liquidity, the pace of settlement, and the visibility of confidence.

The credibility gap, then, is not a bug of stablecoins but their defining feature. It measures the distance between coded certainty and human trust. The wider the gap, the more tempting it becomes to fill it with marketing, attestations, or slogans. Yet only one thing truly closes it: demonstrated convertibility under pressure. The mirror will not lie. When the next run begins—and it will—the question will not be who promised stability, but who proved it.

Why the Periphery Adopts First

On 9 May 2023 in Buenos Aires, the official exchange rate printed one number and every shopkeeper's calculator used another. The peso's annual inflation had vaulted past triple digits, and capital controls meant the formal dollar was a phantom. Freelancers were quoting invoices in stablecoins; small importers settled seed orders in USDT via Telegram; a neighbourhood kiosk on Avenida Rivadavia accepted a QR code for groceries that routed, silently, through a dollar token. The bank was open. The money was leaving. The queue moved too slowly.

The paradox is simple to state and brutal to live. Where the national currency fails as a store of value and bank rails are costly or rationed, people adopt dollar-linked tokens not because a white paper persuaded them, but because rent is due and school fees can't wait. Demand maps to pain. That is why the periphery moves first. It is not a moral judgment; it is a survival tactic.

Show → Name → Explain → Implication. Begin with remittances—the arterial flow of many economies. The World Bank has long tracked how sending money across borders remains expensive and slow relative to policy ambitions, noting the G20's goal to reduce average costs to 3% (World Bank, 2023). In corridors like the Gulf to South Asia and the U.S. to Latin America, families budget weeks around settlement delays and percentage fees that punish the poor. Against that backdrop, a retail worker in Dubai can buy a dollar stablecoin with local currency, push it to a sister in Karachi within minutes, and have her convert to cash through a peer-to-peer market the same afternoon. This is not ideology. It is a measured difference in time and take. The implication is clear: where official rails tax urgency, parallel rails win.

Now name a concrete case that married old and new. In 2022, MoneyGram and Stellar announced a cash-in/cash-out service for USD Coin (USDC) across multiple countries, including the Philippines, allowing users to deposit cash at a counter and receive a dollar stablecoin in a wallet, or reverse the flow and walk out with pesos. Show the behaviour: queues at branches became on-ramps; wallet flows settled near-instantly; cash-out gave finality in the recipient's hand. Explain the mechanism: by stitching a token to the cash economy, the partnership turned remittances into software without stranding the unbanked. Implication: when token rails meet physical exits, adoption follows need, not narrative.

Inflationary contexts tell the same story with different pain. Argentina's National Institute of Statistics and Censuses (INDEC) recorded annual inflation above 100% in 2023. Salaries paid in pesos lost value within days. The visible behaviours were prosaic and decisive: shopkeepers checked the "blue" dollar before pricing; freelancers in Córdoba posted USDT addresses on invoices; small traders used stablecoin savings as an overnight hedge. None of these adopters were chasing yield or speculating on crypto. They were buying time. Each token was a promise that tomorrow's bread would still be priced in something that didn't melt.

Nigeria offers another view of the periphery's logic. The naira's multiple exchange rates and recurrent cash shortages in 2023 pushed ordinary users towards peer marketplaces where dollar tokens priced goods and salaries. Payment processors that historically routed through card networks began to support stablecoin settlements under the hood for merchants serving diaspora customers. Behaviour again over theory: sellers cared whether settlement arrived, not whether it was decentralised; buyers cared whether the exchange spread was fair and predictable, not which chain the token used. The system's morality was functional: it paid on time.

A credible counter-example exists and must be faced. Where domestic payment rails are cheap and ubiquitous, the pressure to adopt stablecoins weakens. India's Unified Payments Interface (UPI), run by the National Payments Corporation of India, routes retail payments at national scale with near-zero marginal cost, settling in seconds across banks. In the UK, Faster Payments achieves similar goals for domestic transfers. When the state and banking sector deliver immediacy and price discipline at home, the periphery logic fails locally. The implication is instructive, not fatal: tokens flourish where gaps persist—in cross-border corridors, in dollarised savings, in grey-market import channels—not where retail pipes already work.

What, precisely, does "pain" measure? It has a receipt. In remittances, it is the margin over the mid-market FX rate, the fixed fee at the counter, and the days until cash-out. In inflation, it is the weekly change in a supermarket basket and the spread between official and street dollars. In access, it is the number of documents required to open an account and the chance a transaction freezes for "enhanced due diligence". Periphery users do not say "I seek a permissionless settlement layer". They say "I must pay school fees by Friday" and choose the rail that makes Friday certain.

Thread a motif through these scenes: the *exit door*. In cracked monetary rooms, people look for exits that work, that open when pushed, and that do not trap them when inspected. Stablecoins offer a cheap key. The key's quality is judged not by academic properties but by how often it snaps under strain. That is why reputations in Lagos and Maracaibo form around spreads and speed, not branding. A wallet that recovers from a locked account in hours, not weeks, earns trust. A counterparty that delivers cash within thirty minutes keeps it.

Two further named examples sharpen the frame. First, Latin America's crypto exchanges that specialise in fiat–stablecoin on- and off-ramps—Bitso in Mexico, Mercado Pago's integrations in Brazil—have wrapped dollar tokens in familiar interfaces. Show: a gig worker in Monterrey receives USDC on a Saturday and cashes out to a local account before dinner at a spread she can predict. Name the actors; explain the flow; implication: tokens gain legitimacy when they hide. Secondly, Turkey during its 2021–2022 inflation surge saw surging retail interest in dollar substitutes, including stablecoins on major exchanges. Internet cafés and phone shops became informal financial outlets, converting lira to USDT and back for small fees. Show the behaviour: queues in Kadıköy at night, Telegram groups with posted rates, receipts photographed against a countertop. Explain: in a context where banks throttle foreign exchange, cash businesses transform into micro-exchanges. Implication: the periphery's adoption engine is entrepreneurial, not institutional.

The periphery also innovates in micro-settlement. In Manila, freelancers on global platforms often invoice in stablecoins to avoid card chargebacks and FX uncertainty, then split receipts across wallets—one for rent, one for family support, one for savings—before converting portions through cash-out partners. This "envelope budgeting" is visible behaviour that token rails accommodate well. The metric is not ideology but misfire rate: how often a withdrawal fails; how high the weekend spread climbs; how quickly a dispute resolves. Where those numbers improve, adoption compounds.

None of this is clean. Tokens rewire power as they solve problems. Informal money changers become critical financial nodes without prudential oversight. Stablecoin issuers, many offshore, become invisible monetary authorities in economies they do not answer to. When a regulator in New York questions a custodian's holdings, a shopkeeper in Rosario learns about counterparty risk the hard way. The periphery takes the first step; it also takes the first fall when something snaps.

A second motif appears: *the cost of certainty*. Users pay in small ways—spreads a touch wider than advertised, cash-out delays when the agent's float runs dry, higher slippage during global volatility. But these costs are linear and legible compared with the step-function risk of a banking freeze or a sudden capital control. The calculus is rational. Pay a visible premium to avoid an invisible cliff. That is the price of certainty when institutions wobble.

The politics of this adoption cannot be wished away. Stablecoins enhance individual agency; they also erode national monetary transmission. When a salary arrives in tokens and stays in tokens until rent is due, the central bank's levers—reserve ratios, moral suasion—do less. Policymakers see leakage; families see survival. Both are right within their frames. The real-world outcome is a blended economy: official rails for taxes, pensions, and utility bills; token rails for savings, remittances, and hedged commerce. In that blend, the dollar's unit of account colonises daily life without a single treaty. The periphery self-dollars as the centre debates.

We need, then, a clear diagnostic to separate hype from habit. Watch four behaviours. First, whether merchants quote prices in local currency but accept stablecoins with a posted spread. Second, whether salary schedules in freelancer communities switch from "wire by Wednesday" to "USDT by Tuesday". Third, whether informal exchanges proliferate near transport hubs—bus stations, ferry terminals—where mobile cash meets human mobility. Fourth, whether capital controls produce "Friday rushes" on token desks before rules change on Monday. Each sighting marks where marketing ends and necessity begins.

A credible limitation must be admitted. Stablecoins do not fix everything. In volatile politics, agents can be harassed; in weak rule-of-law contexts, redemption disputes can become extortion; in heavily sanctioned environments, liquidity dries up at the order of a powerful state. Tokens reduce frictions; they cannot abolish force. The reconciliation is sober. Where institutions are predatory, any rail is an improvement until the same institutions reach it. Where institutions are merely slow, tokens can spur competition and shame upgrades. Either way, the periphery's adoption acts as a stress test for the promises surrounding digital money.

Return to the exit door. Who holds the key when the light flickers? In a healthy adoption pattern, users keep small self-custodied balances for privacy and resilience; cash-out partners are plural; issuers publish timely attestations; regulators focus on exits, not entrances. In an unhealthy pattern, one issuer dominates reserves in one jurisdiction, informal brokers centralise flow, and panic cascades when a rumour hits. The line between the two is not technology. It is governance and redundancy, paid for in quiet times so that doors open in loud ones.

The forward test is blunt. If remittance fees in a given corridor fall and settlement times compress, do households retain the saving or do intermediaries absorb it as margin? If inflation bites harder next quarter, do more salaries settle in tokens by default, and what happens to the local bank's deposit base? If a major issuer's reserves are frozen by a foreign court, can a city's bodega economy switch rails in a week without starving liquidity? These are not thought experiments; they are the questions families and shopkeepers already answer, one payment at a time.

The periphery adopts first because it must. The centre will follow when convenience outweighs comfort, or when the periphery's experiments make escape valves feel normal. Until then, the evidence remains on street corners, chat screens, and shop tills: the exits are open, the costs are counted, and the demand curve traces pain more faithfully than any marketing plan ever could.

Regulation as Moat, Regulation as Muzzle

On 13 February 2023 in New York, the Department of Financial Services directed Paxos to stop issuing BUSD, a dollar stablecoin that had once been the third largest by market capitalisation. The order did not liquidate existing tokens, but it cut the conduit that created new ones. Within days, BUSD's supply began to contract as redemptions outpaced issuance. A single regulatory act had altered market structure more effectively than any rival product. The message travelled quickly through exchanges and chat rooms from Hong Kong to Istanbul: in stablecoins, the most decisive code is sometimes administrative. The licence is a key. It opens. It locks.

Licensing promises safety. It also selects winners. That duality sits at the centre of stablecoin politics. Reserve mandates and redemption rules can prevent the worst failures; they also raise costs, narrow competition, and concentrate power in the few firms that can comply. The motif that will guide this subchapter is the *gate*. Who builds it, who owns it, and who gets to pass through. Gates are not merely legal artefacts; they are design choices that reshape the ledger.

Show → Name → Explain → Implication. Begin with the show. New York's DFS has, since 2015, operated one of the world's most demanding digital-asset regimes. Its stablecoin guidance—updated in 2023—requires 1:1 reserves in cash and cash equivalents, monthly attestations, and clear redemption rights. Name the gatekeeper: NYDFS. Explain the mechanism: by setting stringent reserve quality and disclosure standards, the regulator converts a fragile pledge—"always redeemable"—into a justiciable promise. Implication: coins that pass the gate gain credibility with banks and payment processors; coins that fail lose access to rails. Safety improves. Openness shrinks.

Turn to the European Union. In April 2023, the European Parliament adopted MiCA, a sweeping framework that creates categories for "e-money tokens" and "asset-referenced tokens", sets capital and governance requirements, and caps daily transactions for tokens that could threaten monetary policy. Name the law: Markets in Crypto-Assets Regulation. Explain: MiCA treats fiat-redeemable stablecoins like e-money with stronger guardrails, while constraining large-volume tokens until supervision matures. Implication: legitimacy is granted by statute, not reputation; distribution narrows to firms with cross-border compliance capacity; the voluntary becomes mandatory.

Now a contrasting scene. In December 2023, the Hong Kong Monetary Authority published a consultation proposing that only licensed entities could issue fiat-referenced stablecoins, with full backing in high-quality liquid assets and redemption at par. Name: HKMA's consultation paper. Explain: the city-state seeks to host a "clean" version of the market, tolerating innovation at the edges while anchoring reserves in instruments regulators already understand—Treasuries, cash, and short repos. Implication: the moat deepens. Access for retail remains; access for small issuers diminishes.

Regulation as moat, then, is not a metaphor. It is a budget line. Compliance teams, audit contracts, reserve custodianship, cyber-security certifications—each is a fixed cost only large issuers can absorb. Behaviour reveals the selection: in jurisdictions with tight rules, two or three names dominate issuance; smaller projects either pivot to offshore venues or retreat into the grey. Market concentration rises. The *gate* narrows.

But the moat has a civic logic. It curbs the worst behaviour. Consider Paxos's regulated products contrasted with the algorithmic experiments that collapsed in 2022. Regulated issuers publish attestations, separate reserves, and provide legal redemption rights. Algorithmic issuers promised elastic stability through code. When stress arrived, the former slowed; the latter detonated. A gate that filters collateral quality and redemption mechanics is not paternalism; it is disaster prevention learned from banking history. The implication is hard to evade: if a token claims to be a dollar, the state will eventually demand that it behave like one.

The muzzle appears when gates begin to steer policy through plumbing. The BUSD stop-order showed how a regulator can reshape an entire market by freezing a single issuance source. No protocol was hacked; no private key was lost. Convertibility continued, but only toward zero. This is not an aberration. It is a feature of centralised issuance models that depend on banked reserves and licensed entities. The stabilising power that licensing confers is the same power that can silence a product line overnight—without a court deciding the merits in public. The question is not whether such powers exist; it is how they are bounded, audited, and appealed.

Two named, checkable examples illustrate how regulation both legitimises and centralises. First, Circle's USDC, issued under U.S. state money-transmitter regimes with reserves held in cash and short-dated Treasuries, recovered rapidly from its March 2023 de-peg once U.S. authorities guaranteed Silicon Valley Bank deposits. Show the behaviour: redemptions resumed; the peg restored within days; banks reopened channels. Name the actors: Circle; FDIC; reserve banks. Explain: regulated custody plus transparent reserve composition made it possible for the issuer to re-anchor confidence once the bank backstop returned. Implication: regulation can extend the state's credibility into the token; it can also import the state's crises into it.

Second, the EU's MiCA will, as it phases in, require European-facing issuers to hold authorisations, publish white papers, and maintain prudential buffers. Exchanges will need permissions to list. Show: smaller, crypto-native projects face a choice—restructure as e-money institutions or exit the market. Name: MiCA's authorisation regime. Explain: a measure designed to protect consumers and monetary sovereignty also turns compliance into a competitive moat. Implication: incumbency perks accrue to firms with legal departments and banking relationships. Innovation may move to niches or to non-EU jurisdictions.

A credible counter-example tempers sweeping claims. Some middle-ground regimes use a lighter touch. Singapore's Monetary Authority has, under the Payment Services Act, progressively expanded oversight while allowing pilots under sandbox rules. The approach has produced a market with institutional actors and specialist fintechs both present, and it has attracted banks into tokenised deposit and settlement experiments that do not require public stablecoins at retail scale. The reconciliation is pragmatic: not all gates must be castles. Some can be turnstiles—visible, enforceable, but sized to admit new entrants.

Still, even turnstiles centralise. Reserve rules that require Tier-1 banks as custodians implicitly favour dollar-linked instruments and

U.S. market access. Redemption windows that mandate T+1 settlement incentivise short-duration assets and mature treasury operations. Audit requirements that assume Big Four capacity exclude entities that experiment with on-chain, real-time proofs. The behaviours are measurable: fewer issuers, larger balances per issuer, deeper banking ties, and a migration of functionality off-chain into corporate processes. Each metric says the same thing. Legitimacy scales; openness thins.

The *gate* motif returns with a sharper edge: who writes the gate's API? In practice, the rulebook is co-authored by regulators, large issuers, and large banks. Standards emerge from consultations where only well-resourced parties can contribute substantively. The result is often reasonable—clearer redemption rights, better disclosure—but it bakes incumbents' assumptions into the protocol's periphery. For example, mandating reserve assets exclusively in short-dated sovereign paper improves safety; it also codifies dollar reliance and narrows portfolios to instruments that only large institutions can manage across jurisdictions. The moat deepens at precisely the point where the muzzle becomes plausible.

Consider privacy and access. Where licensing requires deep KYC for even trivial balances, the familiar convenience of cash at small values disappears. The space for anonymous, lawful everyday payments contracts. A regulator can promise proportionality—small transactions with lighter checks, larger ones with scrutiny—but practice often drifts toward uniformity. Why? Because large compliance departments prefer standard procedures, and infrastructure vendors sell uniform toolkits. Behaviour follows incentives. The gate tightens because it is cheaper to tighten once than to calibrate daily.

Now weigh the opposite risk. Without gates, the costs land on the public after failure—through fraud losses, frozen funds, and knock-on damage to payment confidence. The point of reserve rules and licensing is to price those externalities in advance. They work. They also substitute compliance for competition. A market with two or three permitted issuers looks safe. It is also fragile in a new way: each issuer becomes a systemic node, each bank partner a single point of failure, and each regulatory action a macro event. Concentration is not merely economic; it is constitutional.

How should a polity choose? A decision matrix helps only if it forces facts. Measure, do not proclaim. What share of an issuer's reserves sit with a single custodian? How many independent banks hold client cash? What is the maximum daily redemption capacity, by jurisdiction, without relying on central bank emergency windows? How many audits check operational processes versus balance-sheet composition? How long did it take to restore convertibility after the last banking disruption? Answers turn abstractions—trust, resilience, consumer protection—into governance that can be compared and contested.

Two further examples, grounded and checkable, anchor the matrix. First, the Bank of England's statements in 2023 signalled that a regulatory regime for "systemic stablecoins" would apply bank-like standards to issuers whose tokens threaten payment stability, including direct supervision and prudential requirements. Show: the UK aims to admit tokens into mainstream payment chains via familiar oversight. Explain: the approach invites banks to custody reserves and integrate tokens with existing rails. Implication: safety rises; bank dependency deepens; non-bank issuance becomes a narrow niche. Second, Japan's 2023 reforms allowed only licensed banks, trust banks, and certain money transfer agents to issue yen stablecoins, with strict collateral and redemption rules. Show the result: domestic pilots with bank-issued tokens advanced; crypto-native issuers stayed peripheral. Implication: when the gate is bank-shaped, banks walk through.

A credible limitation: over-regulation can drive activity offshore without eliminating risk. When issuers decamp to lenient jurisdictions, users still hold the tokens, and local merchants still accept them. The home regulator then loses both oversight and influence. The reconciliation is to regulate at the *edge*—exchanges, custodians, payment processors—so domestic use meets domestic standards, while leaving room for issuers to experiment under controlled conditions. In other words, place the gate at the city's entrances, not at every doorway.

What, then, of decentralised designs—MakerDAO's Dai or similar—that avoid a corporate issuer? They do not escape the gate; they confront a different one. As those protocols add tokenised Treasuries and bank-like credit exposure to stabilise their pegs, they import off-chain risk and regulatory entanglement piecemeal. Their governance tokens may vote in public; their collateral now depends on jurisdictions, trustees, and tradfi pipes. The muzzle here is subtle: no regulator needs to license the protocol if they can supervise the collateral, the oracles, and the bridges. The gate moves; it does not vanish.

Return once more to the motif. The *gate* is not inherently virtuous or vicious. It is a power. Design it to prevent fraud, preserve convertibility, and protect small users, and it will legitimate the instrument. Design it to throttle entry, pick favourites, or smuggle discretionary policy into plumbing, and it will centralise control while claiming safety. The distinction shows up in defaults. Are holding limits and fees calibrated to prevent bank runs without crippling utility? Are reserve disclosures granular and timely enough to detect duration creep early? Are there redundant banks across jurisdictions, or a single point of political capture? Do small, law-abiding users have a private, low-friction way to transact, or must they submit dossiers to buy groceries?

The forward test is uncomfortable because it is specific. If a major issuer's primary custodian is sanctioned or fails, can redemptions continue at scale through other banks within 72 hours? If a regulator halts new issuance pending a review, can commerce continue without cliff effects? If a new entrant meets reserve and disclosure standards but lacks a household name, can it realistically clear the licensing queue, or is the moat already full? The answers decide whether regulation functions as a public good or as a cartel.

In stablecoins, safety and openness do not merely trade off in theory. They collide in governance. The gate will be built. The only question is whether it is measured by resilience metrics and public rights—or by the comfort of incumbents and the convenience of administrators. Who holds the key is only half the story. Who audits the lock, and who can copy the key when the public interest demands it, will determine whether this market concentrates into fragile safety—or grows into disciplined plurality.

The Dollar Inside the Protocol

On 11 March 2023 in San Francisco, state regulators closed Silicon Valley Bank. By the evening, a dollar stablecoin that prided itself on prudence—USD Coin—traded at eighty-seven cents on major exchanges. The issuer announced that a slice of its reserves sat at the failed bank and that redemptions would resume as soon as access returned. Two days later, after U.S. authorities guaranteed deposits, the peg snapped back. What moved the price was not a smart contract, not a miner, not a validator. It was a statement from the American state. The scene compressed the argument of this subchapter into a single lesson. The dollar lives in the code.

Stablecoins are often marketed as a way to move beyond the banking system. In practice, they are the banking system's most digital emissaries. The overwhelming majority reference the U.S. dollar, hold U.S. dollar assets, and track U.S. dollar money markets through an algorithmic mirror. "Decentralised" money defers to the Federal Reserve's rate path and the U.S. Treasury's bill auctions; on-chain pegs depend on off-chain repo. This is not accidental. It is design. The motif that will guide these pages is the *anchor*: the point where a ledger meets a balance sheet. Follow the anchor and you find that the protocol carries a flag, whether it admits it or not.

Show → Name → Explain → Implication. Begin with reserves. Tether and Circle, issuers of the two most used dollar stablecoins, hold the lion's share of backing assets in cash and short-dated U.S. Treasuries, disclosed through regular attestations. The choice is sensible. Bills are liquid; they price off the world's risk-free curve; they are issued in unfathomable size. The economic reason is obvious; the political consequence is often ignored. When a stablecoin holds U.S. sovereign paper, it internalises American credit as its own safety and American policy as its own limit. If a custody bank freezes, a transfer route closes, or a sanction order touches a counterparty, the on-chain token responds to off-chain jurisdiction. The protocol is faithful. It follows its anchor.

A second example sits in decentralised finance's supposed citadel of neutrality. MakerDAO's Dai began as crypto-collateralised money governed by public votes. As the system matured, risk teams diversified collateral, including tokenised short-term Treasuries and credit exposures through regulated vehicles. The decision reduced volatility and increased capacity. It also reinvented the anchor. Dai's stability now depends partly on the same U.S. credit complex that backs fiat stablecoins; its "neutrality" includes custodians, trustees, and securities law. The implication is not that decentralised experiments are hypocritical. It is that dollar gravity bends even the most careful designs.

Why does the anchor keep drifting back to Washington? Liquidity. The dollar denominates commodities, debt, and much of corporate balance-sheet reality; it is the unit that market makers quote in size at 3 a.m. in Nairobi and 9 a.m. in Seoul. A protocol that promises fast settlement and tight spreads chooses the deepest order book it can find. That book sits in the dollar. Remittances priced in tokens clear faster; they clear in dollars by default. Offshore exchanges settle in seconds; their base pair is a dollar proxy. DeFi's automated market makers display tickers full of crypto symbols, yet their "stable" leg almost always encodes the greenback. The anchor is liquid. So the anchor wins.

Counter-examples exist, and they are instructive. Euro-referenced stablecoins have grown, and some now serve European payments partners with respectable depth. A few projects have launched yen- or gold-linked tokens and attracted niche users hedging local inflation or metal prices. But their volumes remain modest relative to dollar tokens, and their market microstructure reveals thinness: wider spreads, fewer market makers, and episodic liquidity around events rather than round-the-clock depth. The explanation is structural. The euro has substantial real-economy heft but lacks the dollar's capital-market plumbing in some corridors; the yen and bullion have devoted constituencies but not ubiquitous invoicing. Where depth is scarce, pegs are noisy; where pegs are noisy, protocols avoid them. The anchor returns.

Embedding the dollar into code changes the nature of dollar hegemony. In the twentieth century, dominance rested on trade invoicing, reserve holdings, deep bond markets, and global banks with New York correspondent accounts. In the twenty-first, an additional leg has emerged: software that treats the dollar not merely as an instrument but as a default type. Stablecoin libraries, wallet SDKs, and protocol parameter lists include USD as a first-class assumption. Developers in Lagos and Lahore integrate dollar tokens as if they were part of the programming language. The habit is invisible until it isn't. Default becomes doctrine.

The effect is paradoxical. Stablecoins arrived with an anti-friction ethos and an anti-gatekeeper attitude. By replacing clunky bank transfers with programmable settlement, they widened access to something like a dollar account. That access, adopted first in the periphery where inflation bites and remittance fees punish, deepens dollar usage outside the U.S. banking perimeter. A shopkeeper in Rosario never opens a U.S. account, yet she prices stock off a dollar token and pays a wholesaler in a dollar token through a messaging app. A gig worker in Manila pays rent by swapping tokens for cash hours after a global platform releases funds in a dollar proxy. Every such decision grows dollar habit without passing through a bank lobby. The anchor is convenient. Convenience compounds.

The geopolitical inference is straightforward. A money that travels at the speed of APIs multiplies the reach of the policy that governs its reserves. When U.S. regulators compelled reserve transparency and restricted riskier instruments for issuers seeking banking access, the new discipline propagated through tokens that circulate in Nairobi matatus and Buenos Aires kiosks. Conversely, when a U.S. bank failure froze a slice of reserves for a weekend, the shock transmitted to exchanges in Asia by way of a drifting peg. Dollar hegemony softens in form and hardens in function: it feels less like treaties and more like middleware; it still controls the anchor.

Critics object that this analysis overstates dependence and understates optionality. Could not a coalition of non-U.S. central banks develop cross-border corridors that price and settle in their own CBDCs, bypassing the dollar entirely? They can and they are experimenting. Pilots like Project mBridge show that wholesale CBDC platforms can move value atomically across currencies governed by different states. Yet two stubborn hurdles remain. First, invoicing inertia: firms still quote, book, and hedge in dollars. Second, collateral preference: in stress, treasurers flee to U.S. bills the way programmers import standard libraries. Until both shift, on-chain instruments referencing non-dollar rails will struggle to match the speed, size, and certainty of dollar tokens. The anchor is path-dependent.

A quieter objection notes that heavy dollar embedding exposes stablecoins to U.S. policy risk: sanctions, extraterritorial enforcement, and supervisory reach. True. There is muzzle potential in the moat, as the previous section argued. But that risk cuts both ways. The more livelihoods in volatile economies depend on dollar tokens for pay, savings, and trade, the greater the diplomatic cost of blunderbuss enforcement that punishes bystanders. Code stretches the constituency for dollar stability far beyond U.S. voters and bank clients. That constituency has no ballot; it has behaviour. It routes around heavy hands. The anchor earns its keep by being predictable.

To understand how the anchor shapes protocol design, look at fee mechanics and oracle choices in decentralised exchanges. Pricing curves assume a reference asset that is "hard enough" to avoid constant repricing. Oracles that feed prices to lending markets privilege deep, dollar-linked venues because manipulation costs scale with depth. When a lending market accepts a euro token, it often requires higher collateral ratios and tighter liquidation thresholds. This is not cultural bias. It is risk math. The anchor dictates parameters. Those parameters propagate behaviour.

Even experiments that seek to dilute dollar gravity end up measuring themselves against it. A Latin American fintech issues a "digital real" or "digital peso" token for local settlement. It onboards merchants and pays influencers. Behind the scenes, its treasury hedges exposures in dollar tokens and forwards, because investors and suppliers think in dollars. The marketing speaks independence; the risk desk buys dollars quietly. The mirror shows the anchor.

Two further named examples bring the point home. First, the MoneyGram–Stellar cash-to-USDC network, rolled out across dozens of countries, made it possible for people to deposit or withdraw tokenised dollars through a familiar counter. The product's value proposition was not "crypto"; it was "dollars that move like messages". Second, Turkey's 2021–2022 inflation surge saw a proliferation of street-level kiosks and phone shops that bought and sold USDT at posted spreads, effectively functioning as micro-currency boards. In both cases, the protocol's triumph was to embed the dollar where a bank branch did not or could not. The anchor found a new floor.

There is, of course, a ceiling. The more stablecoins concentrate reserves in a narrow set of U.S. custodians and instruments, the more they create single points of failure and political capture. If one or two banks handle most issuer cash, an administrative order can shrink supply overnight. If issuers chase yield up the duration curve during calm, they will sell into gaps during stress. The countermeasure is not mystical decentralisation; it is mundane redundancy—multiple custody banks, multi-jurisdictional structures, conservative ladders, live redemption drills. The anchor must be backed by anchors.

The motif returns one last time. The anchor is a design choice masquerading as a natural law. Protocols could, in principle, embed baskets of currencies, price off synthetic units, or build corridors where non-dollar CBDCs interoperate seamlessly. Some have tried. The market's answer thus far has been blunt: baskets confuse; baskets are illiquid; baskets drift. The dollar is a single number and a deep well. Until alternatives match its immediacy and depth, engineers will keep treating USD as a primitive type. They will keep importing it with a single line of code.

The forward test is therefore not whether a charismatic speech can dethrone hegemony, nor whether a new chain can market neutrality loudly enough. It is whether any non-dollar reference asset can deliver, at scale, the three properties that anchor protocol choice: *depth that resists manipulation*, *ubiquitous quoting in real commerce*, and *legal plumbing that clears crises as swiftly as it clears trades*. If the answer remains no, stablecoins will extend dollar reach even as they decentralise dollar distribution. If the answer becomes yes, the anchor will slip—quietly, then suddenly, ledger by ledger. Until then, the dollar inside the protocol is not a bug. It is the blueprint.

Chapter 6
Designing Freedom — A User's Guide to Monetary Architecture

In October 2022, Nigerian protesters trying to withdraw their own cash discovered that the cash itself had vanished. The central bank's redesign of the naira, coupled with withdrawal limits and network outages, left ATMs dry and digital wallets frozen. People slept outside branches. Traders accepted food in barter. Money existed—but not for them. It was a reminder both old and new: the architecture of finance determines who can move, who must wait, and who may not transact at all. Freedom is not a slogan. It is uptime under duress.

Every monetary system encodes a theory of control. The technical diagrams—nodes, validators, wallets—are political maps drawn in code. Power hides in settings: who can reverse a transaction, who can freeze a balance, who can charge a fee without notice. We inherit systems built for stability, not autonomy, and we design replacements that risk repeating the pattern in more programmable form. Freedom, then, is not an ideology to be declared; it is a set of contingencies to be tested. What remains functional when regulators, insiders, or black swans push every button at once—that is what deserves to be called free.

This chapter takes freedom not as a feeling but as an engineering discipline. The motif is *contact*. How does a monetary architecture behave when it meets the unpredictable—censors, bugs, coups, capital controls, or the quiet corrosion of convenience? Threat models come first because adversaries are honest in their methods. A system that cannot withstand one malicious actor with root access or a single court order that silences a wallet has failed its own premise. In monetary design, freedom that breaks on contact is theatre.

Designing for contact means accepting trade-offs. Privacy layers that protect the innocent also shield the corrupt. Open access can enable crime as easily as creativity. Yet the alternative—perfect compliance through perfect surveillance—produces not safety but stagnation. The task is not to fantasise about absolute freedom, which exists nowhere, but to measure degrees of agency and accountability across architectures. Some freedoms degrade gracefully; others collapse at threshold.

Consider three currencies of exit. The first is *technical*: the ability to fork code or bridge assets when governance fails. The second is *legal*: recourse through courts or contracts that can challenge a confiscation. The third is *practical*: whether ordinary users can migrate their value without prohibitive fees or insider permission. A governance model that cannot be exited is monarchy by dashboard. The ultimate proof of decentralisation is not rhetoric but reversible gravity—when users can leave and the system continues to live.

But exit alone is insufficient without literacy. Privacy, often invoked as virtue, has costs that few articulate. Zero-knowledge proofs, mixers, and stealth addresses are not shields without consequence; they introduce latency, audit friction, and social suspicion. A healthy system teaches *trade-off literacy*—the understanding that privacy is priced, not gifted. Every architecture must answer: how much friction will we pay for dignity? How much visibility for trust? The balances we strike define the politics we practice.

Usability completes the circle. Interfaces are constitutions in disguise. Default options, error messages, recovery flows—each shapes behaviour more powerfully than any manifesto. A system that hides fees centralises advantage in those who read the small print. A wallet that demands technical expertise ensures that power remains with experts. Conversely, design that empowers the novice without infantilising the expert is the rarest public good in digital finance. Simplicity can liberate. It can also deceive.

To grasp this fully, look beyond code to incentives. Developers optimise for retention, regulators for compliance, banks for margin, and users for immediacy. Each goal translates into architecture: recurring prompts for KYC; withdrawal limits to manage liquidity; opaque routing for revenue capture. Each design decision carries politics whether acknowledged or not. The right question is never *whether* systems are political, but *whose* politics they embody.

History repeats through interface. When the Bank of England issued its first notes in 1694, only insiders could redeem them; public trust took decades to form. When PayPal restricted accounts during protests in 2010, the script was familiar: a private actor implementing public policy by design choice. When Tornado Cash was sanctioned in 2022, the tension became explicit—can code itself be a citizen, or is it merely a proxy for those who control it? The answer, as ever, is written in usability and jurisdiction.

Freedom as design discipline forces uncomfortable questions. Should wallets integrate censorship resistance by default or offer toggles for compliance zones? Should bridges enforce identity proofs, or should they treat users as autonomous nodes? Should systems tolerate messy human recovery at the cost of cryptographic purity? These are not academic riddles; they are the constitution-making acts of digital civilisation. Each choice redistributes risk, trust, and power. Each produces winners invisible to those who never had options to begin with.

This chapter approaches these dilemmas as a manual for citizens, not consumers. You will encounter frameworks for evaluating threat models, understanding exit mechanisms, assessing privacy's real costs, and reading user interfaces as political texts. The intent is not to prescribe ideal blueprints but to cultivate diagnostic habits: to see where design protects agency and where it quietly erodes it. Once you learn to read architecture as argument, you will never look at a payment rail—or a policy document—the same way again.

The test of any monetary system is simple: what happens when you disagree with it? Freedom that requires permission is dependency by another name. True design maturity lies not in preventing dissent but in surviving it. The coming pages trace how that survival can be engineered—how code, law, and culture might converge to keep systems open when every incentive pulls them closed. The question that threads through all that follows is deceptively small and endlessly radical: when contact comes, will your money still move?

Threat Models First

On 5 February 2022, in Ottawa, Canada, the federal government invoked emergency powers to freeze the bank accounts of protest organisers and anyone who had donated more than a few hundred dollars to their cause. Payment processors complied within hours; major banks followed with precision. One crowdfunding platform, GoFundMe, halted transfers citing "policy violations", while another, GiveSendGo, suffered a data breach that exposed thousands of donor names. It was not a coup or a market crash that paralysed those involved—it was the plumbing of finance itself. Money moved only where permission was granted. The lesson was unambiguous: the true test of a monetary system is not how it performs in prosperity, but how it behaves when contested.

Every credible design begins with its enemies. Freedom without a threat model is decoration; security without imagination is theatre. Monetary systems have always been adversarial environments, and yet digital engineers often forget that the quietest failure is not a bug or a hack but a silent exclusion. Who can be censored? Where are the chokepoints? Which insiders can be compromised? Which black swans could collapse the chain? These questions define whether an architecture sustains liberty or merely rehearses it. The motif that will guide this section is the *mirror*. Only by looking at our adversaries do we see our own assumptions reflected.

Threat modelling starts from the premise that risk is not abstract. It is embodied—in the regulator who overreaches, the contractor who misconfigures a node, the market maker who loses liquidity, or the insider who trades privileged information. Each represents a vector not of technology but of trust. Show, name, explain, imply: when Binance suspended withdrawals for hours in June 2021 after a surge in activity, the technical message was "temporary congestion". The human message was fragility. A single point of control, however efficient, becomes a single point of failure under pressure. The implication is architectural: resilience requires redundancy; redundancy requires accepting inefficiency. Freedom trades elegance for survivability.

Contrast that with Bitcoin's decentralised topology during the same period. No single authority could pause redemptions; no participant could coerce a global stop. Yet this robustness came at a cost—slow settlement, volatile fees, and limited adaptability. The mirror reveals trade-offs, not heroes. Centralised systems fail loudly and recover quickly; decentralised ones degrade slowly and recover through collective improvisation. The designer's task is not to pick a side but to calibrate exposure. How much control buys convenience before it sells out freedom?

Censorship remains the oldest and most visible adversary. It wears many uniforms: government decree, private moderation, compliance error. When Visa and Mastercard suspended service to WikiLeaks in December 2010 after diplomatic pressure from Washington, the site did not disappear—but its funding did. The incident inspired a wave of donations through Bitcoin, marking the first major test of censorship resistance as a public good rather than a novelty. The system's response revealed its asymmetry: small actors could survive by routing around gatekeepers, but scaling that resistance required tools ordinary users could not yet wield. The mirror showed both promise and exclusion. Resilience was real; usability was not.

Chokepoints evolve faster than ideology. The move toward digital compliance has collapsed thousands of payment corridors into a handful of global rails. SWIFT, Fedwire, CHIPS—each serves billions through a few dozen institutions. The same concentration recurs in crypto's custody layer, where a small cluster of exchanges and stablecoin issuers handle the majority of volume. When one fails, as FTX did in November 2022, contagion spreads not through code but through balance sheets. The implication is sobering: decentralisation on paper can conceal centralisation in practice. A thousand wallets may depend on one API key.

Insiders form the most insidious class of adversary because they operate inside the perimeter of trust. Rogue administrators, compliant legal teams, captured auditors—all have the capacity to turn private systems into instruments of control. The 2016 Bitfinex breach was not the work of cryptographic failure but compromised operational processes; the 2023 revelation that certain exchange employees shared client data with law enforcement without warrants showed that the gate can always be opened from within. Design that assumes virtue is an invitation to abuse. Systems must be built to tolerate bad faith, not to reward it.

Then there are black swans: improbable, system-wide events that expose hidden correlations. When the TerraUSD stablecoin collapsed in May 2022, it erased over $40 billion in nominal value within days. What began as a technical arbitrage loop became a liquidity death spiral that stressed the wider market. The chain did not need to be attacked to fail; it needed only to meet its own assumptions under strain. Black swans are mirrors that show complacency. They remind designers that models built in calm seas cannot predict storms.

Every threat model reveals its own design doctrine. Censors demand redundancy; chokepoints demand interoperability; insiders demand transparency and least privilege; black swans demand circuit breakers and humility. Freedom is not the absence of threats but the capacity to function while surrounded by them. The crucial metric is *degradation curve*: how fast does a system lose integrity when one component misbehaves? Can a wallet still redeem value when APIs fail? Can a bridge reroute when an oracle goes dark? Can governance execute emergency code without centralising authority? Freedom measured at uptime is illusion; freedom measured at failure is truth.

Some argue that robust threat models hinder innovation. They slow deployment, invite paranoia, and deter mainstream adoption. There is merit in the objection. Excessive hardening can strangle usability, while perpetual suspicion corrodes collaboration. Yet the counterfactual—designing for the sunny day—is worse. History's most catastrophic financial losses stem from optimism untested by imagination: the 2008 mortgage crisis, born of models that ignored tail risk; the 2022 algorithmic stablecoin crash, born of faith in equilibrium. The reconciliation lies in discipline. A credible system distinguishes between paranoia and preparedness through rehearsal: simulated attacks, audit transparency, live stress tests. What the military calls "red teaming", monetary designers must make routine.

The mirror returns in governance. Who defines the threat model? In most systems, the same actors who stand to lose least from failure—

executives, regulators, or core developers. This asymmetry breeds fragility because the incentives to imagine catastrophe decline as stakes rise. True resilience emerges only when the model includes those at the edges: the merchant who cannot withdraw, the migrant whose remittance is frozen, the developer who cannot fork without legal risk. Freedom requires plural imagination. Only adversarial empathy can anticipate adversarial power.

Two examples illustrate this principle. In 2019, the Hong Kong protests prompted mass withdrawals and the use of digital payment alternatives when authorities began tracing transactions. Local activists shifted to prepaid cards and peer-to-peer swaps, a primitive but functional threat response. In contrast, during the Nigerian naira redesign crisis of 2023, centralised mobile money systems buckled under demand because no redundant architecture existed outside official channels. Both crises revealed the same pattern: where users had multiple exit routes, coercion lost leverage; where they did not, liquidity became loyalty. The implication is architectural, not ideological. Freedom is not declared; it is engineered.

A credible counter-example tempers absolutism. Sweden's near-cashless economy functions with high trust and minimal censorship. Citizens rely almost entirely on bank apps and instant payment systems like Swish without systemic abuse. The absence of adversarial behaviour allows efficiency to dominate design. Yet this model scales poorly beyond culturally homogeneous, high-trust societies. Transplant it to fractured polities and it becomes brittle. The reconciliation is contextual: systems can afford centralisation only when social capital substitutes for cryptographic defence. Threat models are local mirrors reflecting cultural assumptions.

The motif of the mirror culminates in self-inspection. Every designer, policymaker, or investor should ask: who benefits from my system's failure? Who could exploit my own convenience? What single point, if removed, would silence an entire community? These questions replace slogans with diagnostics. They force the recognition that censorship resistance, auditability, and redundancy are not ideological luxuries—they are survival traits.

The forward test remains open. Suppose a government demands that all stablecoin issuers implement real-time surveillance hooks. Suppose a key custodian disappears in bankruptcy. Suppose a protocol's oracle is captured by a state actor. Which parts of the network continue to function, and which require mercy to restart? That is the measure of freedom. It is not what a system promises when trusted, but what it preserves when betrayed. The mirror never lies. It only waits for contact.

Governance You Can Actually Exit

On 1 August 2017, a group of miners, companies, and users split Bitcoin into two networks over a single parameter: block size. Exchanges from Hong Kong to Zurich listed "Bitcoin Cash" as a distinct asset; wallets issued replay protection; hash power reshuffled within hours. The outcome was messy, public, and permanent: two communities, two chains, two economic histories from one code base. Exit was not a manifesto; it was a transaction. Exit must be operational, always.

The paradox is clear. Most projects speak of choice; few enable it at the speed of loss. Exit should not mean waiting for a court's mercy or a help desk's reply. It should be a button, a script, a path you can walk when you disagree with governors or when governors fail. This subchapter argues that "governance you can exit" is not a slogan about freedom; it is a measurable property defined by four surfaces: forks, bridges, custody mobility, and legal recourse. Think of it as a building's fire exit. You do not admire it daily. You test it before the smoke.

Show → Name → Explain → Implication. Begin with forks. The 2016 DAO crisis on Ethereum—when a vulnerability drained millions of ether from a high-profile fund—culminated in a chain split in July 2016 after an on-chain and off-chain debate that involved core developers, miners, and exchanges. The fork reversed the theft; a minority rejected the edit and continued as Ethereum Classic. Forks expose the bare metal of exit: the ability to carry your rules and your ledger with you when a majority takes a path you will not follow. But a fork is not freedom if you cannot bring along users, developers, and infrastructure. The implication is practical. Forkability must be paired with viability.

Forks are rare because they are expensive. They fracture liquidity, split tooling, and confuse newcomers. That is precisely why they work as last-resort governance. People fork only when compelled. Real optionality lives earlier and more often in bridges—the connective tissue across chains and custody platforms. Bridges let communities relocate assets without restarting civilisation. When built well, they convert ideological schisms into logistics, not purges.

Yet bridges are also risk concentrators. The Wormhole exploit in February 2022, which drained wrapped assets before the backer recapitalised the hole, showed how an exit corridor can become a breach point. The Ronin bridge hack in March 2022, tied by investigators to state-backed actors, underlined that centralised validators turn "bridges" into vault doors with too few keys. The lesson is sobering: exit channels must be survivable under attack, not just convenient in peacetime. If the fire exit is nailed shut by design, you do not have governance. You have stage dressing.

Custody mobility is the next surface. Mobility means that you can move your assets and keys across providers and jurisdictions without begging. It is measured, not declared: how many clicks to export a seed? How many days to clear a withdrawal under stress? How many independent custody routes exist if your primary provider fails? Set these as targets and watch behaviours change. When FTX froze withdrawals in November 2022, users learnt that platform "governance" without an exit was theatre; balances on a screen were opinions, not rights. By contrast, when a hardware wallet maker in May 2023 proposed a cloud recovery service that split key shards with third parties, the backlash was not technophobia but an argument about mobility: an exit you cannot verify is not an exit you can trust.

Legal recourse anchors the last surface. Code is not law when servers, banks, and people sit behind it. Law is law. It matters whether your claim on a custodian is a segregated trust right or an unsecured IOU; whether a court can order restitution; whether your jurisdiction recognises self-custody as possession. The Mt Gox rehabilitation through the Tokyo District Court after its 2014 collapse has been glacial and procedural, yet it has also demonstrated that paper rights can eventually move money. Legal recourse is slow. It is still exit. Measure it. Design for it.

The motif throughout is the *fire exit*. Not the grand staircase used on gala nights, but the quiet door that opens away from smoke. Forks are the back stairwell; bridges the corridor that leads to it; custody mobility the handle that turns; legal recourse the outside latch if all else jams. In each case, exit becomes a verb when two things hold: you can act without permission from the party you are leaving, and others can recognise your action as legitimate.

Let's apply the engine to each surface, pairing abstraction with behaviour.

Forks: Show the precedent. Bitcoin Cash in 2017, Ethereum/Ethereum Classic in 2016. Name the behaviours that matter: replay protection to prevent cross-chain theft; exchange listings that honour user choice; client diversity so no single implementation dictates outcome. Explain the core idea: fork feasibility equals bargaining power. It disciplines governance because any majority must win consent, not simply win votes. Implication: communities that can credibly separate negotiate better rules before they must. Where forking is impossible in practice—because one company holds the code, or one exchange controls the order book—governance degenerates into decree masked as consensus.

Bridges: Show the duality. They are exits and entrances. Name the constraint: security assumptions. The more a bridge relies on a handful of signers, the more your "exit" depends on their keys, not your agency. Explain the design space: light-client bridges that verify proofs on each side; optimistic bridges with fraud windows; multi-party computation for signer sets. Implication: a project should state plainly which bridges it trusts, with what caps, and why. If those answers are marketing, not engineering, your "exit" is a hall of mirrors.

Custody mobility: Show simple tests. Can a non-expert export keys without cloud services? Can a business move from custodian A to custodian B with a defined service-level objective and no hidden fees? Can a user survive a SIM-swap attack because recovery options require in-person verification rather than a helpful email? Name the metrics: time-to-withdrawal during a provider outage; percentage of assets in cold storage with independent recovery paths; number of supported signing clients. Explain the politics: interfaces that hide key export, or charge punitive exit fees, centralise power in "customer success" departments. Implication: mobility is governance from below. Providers that fear it fear their users.

Legal recourse: Show the contrast. A New York trust charter for a stablecoin issuer gives holders a right against segregated assets; a generic money transmitter licence may not. Name the mechanics: jurisdictions with clear frameworks for digital assets as property (England and Wales have advanced case law; Singapore has built pragmatic pathways) versus jurisdictions that treat tokens solely as black boxes. Explain the constraint: legal exit is jurisdiction-bound and slow, but it prevents the worst form of capture—private law written in user agreements. Implication: hold claims where judges can read them.

Two named, checkable examples tie these threads. First, the New York Agreement of May 2017, a meeting of companies at the offices of Digital Currency Group that attempted to coordinate a "SegWit2x" change to Bitcoin. The agreement faltered by November; the hard fork was cancelled. Why? Because node operators and users could credibly refuse to run the software. Exit disciplined governance without a split. The fire exit existed; its mere presence changed behaviour. Second, the July 2016 Ethereum decision to fork after The DAO exploit. Exchanges had to decide which chain to list. Many listed both. Users were not trapped in a single truth, even if the politics were bruising. Fork feasibility converted governance from edict into choice.

A credible counter-example must be admitted. There are contexts where exit fragments public goods. Repeated forking can splinter security budgets, confuse non-technical users, and invite opportunists to replay old histories for profit. Bridges multiply failure domains and create honeypots. Custody mobility can expose users to phishing if recovery flows are too permissive. Courts can turn into chokepoints if a powerful jurisdiction asserts extraterritorial control. The reconciliation is not to abandon exit but to price it. Exit should be costly enough to deter frivolity and cheap enough to deter tyranny. That price lives in friction: timelocks for upgrades, cooling-off periods for bridges, staged withdrawals for large accounts, jurisdictional diversification for reserves.

So, how does one measure real optionality? Set discipline into checklists that bite. For forks: count independent client implementations; track how often they pass consensus tests; record how quickly security patches propagate across them. For bridges: publish caps by asset and chain; rotate signers across geographies and legal entities; prove liveness through regular drills that simulate signer loss. For custody mobility: compute the median time to full exit for retail and institutional users; test recovery with red teams; guarantee no-fee key export. For legal recourse: map which claims attach to which assets; calculate time to injunction when a custodian fails; disclose which courts can compel action. Numbers convert ideals into governance.

Return to the fire exit. Who inspects it? Exit that depends on benevolent gatekeepers is not exit. Communities must institutionalise scepticism. Exchanges should pre-commit to listing policies that do not punish principled forks. Wallets should adopt recovery standards that do not bind users to one vendor. Protocol teams should document what would constitute an intolerable change—and how dissenters would depart with dignity. Courts should publish predictable pathways for property claims in digital contexts. Auditors should time withdrawals, not just balance sheets.

The hardest part is cultural. Users prefer comfort until it hurts. Engineers prefer elegance until it snaps. Regulators prefer order until it stifles exit so completely that failure becomes systemic. Governance you can actually exit asks each to accept discomfort in peacetime to avoid catastrophe in wartime. It is a discipline of drills, not declarations.

The forward test is concrete. If a dominant bridge in your ecosystem fails tonight, can value reach safety tomorrow through another path? If your custody provider is enjoined by a court, can your business operate using self-hosted keys within forty-eight hours? If core developers adopt a change you cannot accept, can your community credibly continue with patches, peers, and listings? If a stablecoin you rely on freezes assets in your jurisdiction, can you settle obligations through alternatives without bankrupting counterparties? These are not hypotheticals for a distant future. They are the daily diagnostics of a free monetary life.

Exit remains the only governance right that guarantees the rest. When exit is a verb, promises become contracts, and contracts become habits. When it is not, all that remains is trust without leverage. A system worth living under does not demand that faith. It earns it, door by door, drill by drill, until the day comes when smoke fills the stairwell and you turn a handle that opens.

Privacy without Delusion

On 8 August 2022 in Washington, D.C., the U.S. Treasury's Office of Foreign Assets Control sanctioned Tornado Cash smart contracts. Within hours, front-end interfaces geofenced users; major relays on Ethereum's MEV-Boost stack began filtering transactions that touched sanctioned addresses; GitHub briefly removed the project's repositories. Days later in Amsterdam, Dutch authorities arrested a developer on suspicion of facilitating money laundering. Code had met policy. The outcome was not theoretical. It was a live demonstration that *programmable* money inherits *programmable* surveillance. Real privacy is never free.

The paradox arrived in plain sight: a tool built to shield legitimate user flows from indiscriminate tracking became a target because it could also hide crime. That tension is not a footnote; it is the subject. Effective privacy resists dragnet scrutiny. Effective privacy also constrains forensic reconstruction after harm. Any serious design must price both facts. The motif of this subchapter is the *receipt*: every layer of privacy leaves one—paid in fees, latency, complexity, reputational risk, or political capital. The receipt may be small in peacetime. It grows during crisis.

Show → Name → Explain → Implication. Start with the most familiar privacy claim in public ledgers: pseudonymity. Bitcoin's addresses look anonymous. They are not. Clustering heuristics link them with high accuracy using change-address patterns, timing analysis, and exchange KYC data. Firms such as Chainalysis and Elliptic built entire businesses on those heuristics. The explanation is mechanical: transparent ledgers plus behavioural regularities yield identities. The implication is uncomfortable: base-layer pseudonymity protects almost no one against a motivated investigator. If your adversary includes a bank, an exchange, or a state, the receipt for "privacy by obscurity" is paid later—at indictment or asset freeze.

Next, name a cryptographic answer: Zcash, launched in 2016, introduced zk-SNARKs to shield sender, receiver, and amount. Usage, however, concentrated in transparent addresses for years. Why? The receipt. Shielded transactions were heavier, slower on some clients, and difficult to integrate across exchanges and wallets. After the Sapling upgrade (2018) made proofs lighter, adoption improved, yet liquidity remained split between shielded and transparent pools. The design lesson is clear. If privacy costs users usability or speed, most will not pay the receipt unless compelled. Privacy you must go out of your way to use is privacy that, at scale, will fail.

Monero took another path: ring signatures and stealth addresses by default, with RingCT hiding amounts. This choice pushed the receipt into validator load and transaction size, and into the politics of exchange listings. Some venues delisted Monero under compliance pressure; others kept it with heightened monitoring. Again the trade-off is visible. Make privacy the default and you burden infrastructure and liquidity access; make it optional and you stratify users into those who blend and those who stand out. There is no neutral ground. The receipt is always attached.

Programme the lens wider. Privacy in programmable money has at least four layers: *network* (who talks to whom), *transaction* (what fields are visible), *application* (what a dApp records), and *institutional edge* (what exchanges, merchants, or banks see). Each layer offers tools. For networks: Tor, mixnets, transaction broadcast through privacy-preserving servers. For transactions: mixers, shielded pools, confidential transactions, stealth addresses. For applications: data minimisation, differential privacy on analytics. For the edge: cash-like "offline small payments" and tiered thresholds proposed in some central-bank pilots. Each tool prints a receipt: slower propagation, higher fees, false positives on compliance screens, or limited feature sets. The designer's task is to choose which receipt the user can most afford to pay.

Consider a specific, checkable episode. After OFAC's action in August 2022, a significant share of Ethereum blocks—built via compliant relays—excluded transactions interacting with sanctioned contracts. Censorship at the relay layer did not render the network unusable, but it did fragment mempools and extended confirmation times for some users. Show the behaviour: higher variance in inclusion, longer waits for tainted flows, workarounds via self-built blocks or non-censoring relays. Explain: even without base-layer censorship, *infrastructure centralisation* creates soft chokepoints. Implication: privacy that relies on the goodwill of a small number of operators is privacy with a quorum. A quorum can be leaned on.

A credible counter-example argues that privacy can coexist with accountability through selective disclosure. Zero-knowledge proofs, when engineered well, allow a user to prove compliance with a rule—"I'm in good standing", "this amount is below a threshold", "these funds are not blacklisted"—without exposing raw data. Projects in the payment space and some central-bank prototypes have trialled "tiered privacy", where small transactions remain offline or pseudonymous, and larger ones require additional proofs. The reconciliation is pragmatic, not utopian. Selective disclosure moves the receipt from surveillance to cryptographic cost and operational complexity. If proofs are slow or APIs clumsy, businesses will quietly disable them. If they are fast and standards-based, norms can shift.

Pair abstractions with behaviours. *Trust* shows up as a merchant choosing to accept a privacy-enhanced payment because dispute workflows exist and chargeback rates are clear. *Efficiency* shows up as confirmation targets that remain under a minute despite privacy overhead. *Risk* shows up as the proportion of false positives in compliance screens—misflagged addresses per thousand—and the average time to clear them. Publish these metrics, and privacy stops being a vibe. It becomes a service quality property with a measurable receipt.

Blinded signatures and e-cash deserve attention as well. Chaumian mints—revived in modern, federated forms—enable cash-like tokens with strong unlinkability and server-enforced issuance rules. Their receipt is custodian risk and federation governance: you gain anonymity against outsiders, but you must trust a quorum not to inflate or deanonymise. In settings where small private payments are socially valuable—journalism, health, political organising—this may be a fair price. In others, it will not be. The point is choice with eyes open.

The social costs of privacy need naming without euphemism. Strong financial privacy also shelters fraud, extortion, and tax evasion. Communities pay when scammers vanish behind mixers; states pay when corruption launders funds unnoticed; markets pay when asymmetric information becomes a weapon. Yet dragnet surveillance imposes social costs too: self-censorship, discriminatory targeting, chilling effects on dissent, data breaches that never heal. Pretending either side is costless is delusion. Trade-off literacy starts by reading *both* receipts.

Two governance examples show how societies try to price these costs. First, the European debate on a digital euro explored "offline small payments" with privacy closer to cash for modest amounts, and standard compliance for larger transactions, together with technical designs that keep the central bank blind by default. The receipt for citizens is capped anonymity; the receipt for the state is bounded investigative delay. Second, the Financial Action Task Force's "travel rule" guidance (2019 onward) pushed virtual-asset providers to exchange sender and recipient information above thresholds. The receipt for users is less frictionless movement between custodial venues; the receipt for firms is compliance overhead that large players absorb more easily than small ones, with centralising effects. These are political choices encoded in code paths.

Usability decides whether privacy survives contact. Interfaces that bury privacy options three menus deep make a moral decision look like a personal failing. Wallets that default to transparent transactions while advertising "privacy ready" will produce users who intend privacy and achieve none. Conversely, defaults that pick privacy for small payments—and explain what changes for larger transfers—teach habits without sermons. An honest receipt in UI form says: "This transfer will cost £0.42 more and may take one additional block; in exchange, your counterparty and observers cannot link this payment to your prior receipts." Users can then decide. Designers must commit.

The *receipt* motif returns with institutional edges. Merchants, exchanges, and fintechs face reputational receipts for touching flows that later prove criminal, even when they followed best practice. Their predictable response is over-compliance: block first, appeal later. That creates its own harm. Clearing a false positive in hours rather than weeks must become a performance target—publicly audited—to keep privacy from being strangled by process. Numbers discipline fear.

Hidden receipts lurk in data exhaust. Analytics libraries inside wallets and dApps record clicks and balances unless carefully minimised; push notifications leak timing; cloud backups reveal seed fragments to third parties. A privacy-preserving protocol wrapped in a garrulous app is no longer privacy-preserving. The fix is tedious and necessary: local analytics, opt-in telemetry, encrypted backups with user-held keys, and deletion guarantees that are real and tested. This is not marketing. It is plumbing.

A second counter-example to absolutism: some societies function well with minimal financial privacy because social trust, legal norms, and welfare states cushion the harms of visibility. Sweden's reliance on Swish and bank apps illustrates a world where near-total traceability has not obviously crushed civil liberty. But context matters. Transplant that model to a fragile state and surveillance becomes a weapon within weeks. Trade-off literacy must be local. The receipt is always denominated in a society's actual institutions, not in universal ideals.

So what counts as privacy without delusion? Three properties: *bounded promises*, *visible costs*, and *credible fallbacks*. Bounded promises say what the system shields and from whom—network observers, counterparties, intermediaries—and what it cannot. Visible costs show users the fee, delay, or feature loss that buys privacy. Credible fallbacks define what happens when a layer fails: if a mixer is sanctioned, can users reclaim funds; if a wallet ceases support for shielded pools, can users migrate; if a federation fractures, can members redeem claims. Deliver these, and privacy becomes a civic technology, not a slogan.

The forward test is plain. If a government mandates tighter reporting, can your system preserve small-value private payments by design? If a major relay cluster begins censoring, can users route around it without becoming engineers? If an exchange delists a privacy coin, can merchants still take it with acceptable spreads? If a breach exposes a compliant mixer's database, does your counterparty learn anything beyond that a payment occurred? Each answer is a receipt. Collect them and you own your choices.

Privacy worthy of a free society does not promise invisibility. It promises proportion. It does not confuse anonymity with impunity or transparency with virtue. It makes trade-offs teachable and defaults humane. It prices the costs where they belong—at the margin of larger payments, at the point of institutional scrutiny—while keeping ordinary dignity cheap. The receipt remains. The question is whether we demand to see it, read it together, and pay it with intent rather than with regret.

Usability as Politics

In May 2023, the Paris-based hardware wallet maker Ledger announced "Ledger Recover", a paid feature to split an encrypted fragment of a user's secret key and store shards with third parties. The goal was humane—help people who lose seed phrases. The reaction was ferocious. Forums lit up; developers published threat models; customers filmed themselves destroying devices. No statute had changed. No consensus rule had moved. A single opt-in toggle in a settings panel had reallocated trust from the user's pocket to a vendor's cloud. The button made policy visible.

Interfaces are constitutions disguised as convenience. They allocate power by deciding what is explicit, what is buried, and what is impossible. They decide who sees the fee and who doesn't; who can recover a key and at what price; who can send now and who must wait for a review. We speak of "UX" as if it were merely decoration. It is not. Defaults govern before any law arrives. A green checkmark makes compliance feel like choice; a greyed-out button converts a rule into a habit. When money is software, the person who designs the screen writes the first draft of policy.

Show → Name → Explain → Implication. Begin with defaults. In January 2021, at the height of the GameStop volatility, the brokerage app Robinhood limited buying in certain securities and left the sell button active. The company cited clearinghouse deposit requirements; engineers scrambled to meet collateral calls. Yet to the user, the political reality was the interface: one option available, the other not. A decision by a risk engine and a compliance team manifested as a one-sided screen. The implication is not that all risk controls are wrong; it is that a default can become a veto without debate when it arrives as UI.

Defaults are power because they are invisible. Toggle off private memoranda by default and most people will never find them; toggle on "share data to improve service" and most will never question it. In money, default fee levels, default gas limits, default slippage tolerances, default memo fields, default key-backup settings—each is a throttle or a trap. They determine who pays, who waits, and who fails. They also determine who is blamed, because human beings assume that what an interface offers is what is allowed.

Fee visibility is the most common site of quiet capture. The difference between an honest wallet and an extractive one is often a single line: "You will pay £X; the protocol takes £Y; your provider earns £Z." Many products show the first and hide the rest behind "network fees", a phrase that folds spread, convenience mark-ups, and affiliate cuts into a single innocent total. Name the behaviour, then measure it: the effective spread over mid-market FX, the proportion of fee revenue captured by the app, the frequency with which "priority" fees are suggested during peak congestion. Explain the politics: an interface that trains users to accept opaque costs is a tax farm with animated gradients. The implication is that transparency is not a virtue signal; it is a check on rent.

Key recovery is where usability's mercy can become its quiet coup. Ledger's proposal split secrets with custodians to help ordinary people who lose phrases. That is a real pain, not a contrivance. It also creates a new attack surface and a new category of compliance hook: court orders for shard custodians, insider abuse at the recovery providers, misconfigurations that leak metadata about who opted in. Interfaces in this space must state the trade with ruthless clarity: what is encrypted, who holds fragments, which jurisdictions can compel, how to opt out—and how to exit later. If a recovery flow cannot be explained without euphemism, the design is not humane; it is paternal.

Consider a second, opposite case. In 2007, Safaricom launched M-Pesa in Nairobi with USSD menus and agents at kiosks. The interface was the simplest possible list of actions: send, withdraw, deposit. No seed phrases. No sliders. No slippage. The politics were just as profound: a private company and a regulator blessed a rail that made inclusion cheap for millions, while centralising power in a single operator. Usability here emancipated and concentrated at once. The implication is sobering. Simplicity can be liberty for users and leverage for providers. Both facts are true at once.

Interfaces are also where censorship hides. In August 2022, after the U.S. Treasury sanctioned Tornado Cash contracts, some major Ethereum relays began filtering blocks that included sanctioned interactions. The network continued to operate, but the experience shifted. Wallets that routed through censoring infrastructure produced longer waits or puzzling failures. Websites geofenced code; RPC providers quietly enforced policies that never saw a parliamentary vote. The compliance decision was infrastructural; its reality was a spinner that spun too long. If censorship never shows up as "blocked by law" but as "network error, please try again", citizens cannot meaningfully contest it.

The motif for this subchapter is the *toggle*. Not a metaphorical one. The literal toggle that sits next to "fast" or "private", "recover" or "self-custody", "convert" or "withdraw". The toggle is the hinge where products choose sides. It is the place to interrogate power: who set the default; who benefits if it remains; who suffers if it flips; who can change it; who can't. Follow the toggle and you will find the constitution.

Pair abstractions with behaviours. *Trust* is not a word in a brand deck; it is a pattern in support tickets: how many users successfully recover funds without insider assistance; how many can export keys without touching the cloud; how often are disputes resolved within 48 hours. *Efficiency* is not a claim in a keynote; it is the median taps to complete a cross-border transfer, and the variance in completion time during congestion. *Risk* is not a vague sense of dread; it is the ratio of failed sends to total sends when a provider's primary relay cluster is degraded, and the percentage of transactions that fall back to an uncensored path.

Bridges and cross-chain tools expose usability's constitutional role. A "bridge" button that defaults to the cheapest centralised route tempts users into honeypots; a bridge that puts light-client routes up front, with caps and warnings for trusted paths, distributes risk more honestly. After the Wormhole exploit in February 2022 and the Ronin bridge compromise in March 2022, responsible interfaces learned to annotate routes with security assumptions. The politics here are specific: *which* risks are normalised for novices, and *which* are placed behind an explicit "I accept" wall. Interfaces either discipline greed or amplify it.

Some argue that surfacing all this complexity will cost adoption. They have a point. Walls of warnings paralyse. But minimalism that hides consequence is not humane; it is exploitative. The reconciliation is design craft: progressive disclosure that keeps the first screen simple without lying about costs; plain-English receipts for fees and risks; defaults that protect the small and demand intention from the large. A "small, private payment" mode that is *on by default* below a threshold teaches freedom; a hidden switch teaches nothing.

CBDC pilots sharpen the stakes. If a public wallet defaults to "expiry enabled" for relief funds, that one setting normalises programmable purchasing power in a way that will be hard to reverse. If the offline mode requires a central server handshake every week, the "cash-like" promise is theatre. If fee schedules bury negative remuneration inside "service charges", the political cost of policy disappears behind UX. Conversely, a wallet that prints the fine print in the flow—*expiry is off by default; category blocks require law; offline small payments keep the central bank blind*—uses interface to bind the state. The constitution has a UI.

Private platforms play the same game. A stablecoin app that auto-selects its own market maker for swaps without showing the spread is enacting a tax by design. A broker that turns off "buy" and leaves "sell" on during stress is enacting a capital control by design. A KYC flow that refuses passports from certain countries without stating a legal basis is enacting a blacklist by design. None of these are mere UI choices. They are governance choices with human costs.

Key recovery, again, reveals the sharpest knife. Recovery flows that rely on biometric scans and cloud escrow reassign sovereignty to vendors, because the failure mode becomes "prove yourself to us" rather than "prove yourself to you". Recovery flows that use social guardians or time-locked vaults place power with the user's chosen circle, at the cost of social complexity and the risk of collusion. Recovery flows that rely on multisig with geographically distributed co-signers reduce single-jurisdiction capture at the cost of coordination. The toggle embodies a political theory of the person: subject of a platform, member of a community, or self-administering agent. Any flow that pretends to avoid that choice is selling comfort as ideology.

A credible counter-example tempers zeal. There are contexts where paternal defaults save lives: rate limits that prevent fat-fingered millions, anti-phishing delays on first use, cooldowns on large withdrawals from new devices. These are, strictly speaking, frictions. They are also, done well, constitutional guarantees for the novice against predators. The critical test is whether the power to bypass them exists and is legible. A professional desk must be able to opt into a faster path with published SLAs and visible insurance, not secret relationships. A citizen must be able to unlock small, private payments without a customer-service interrogation. A journalist must be able to hold a modest balance without a marketing profile built from their spend.

Turn the motif once more. The toggle is a lie detector. Ask it questions. What is the default gas strategy and who profits? Which path is recommended for bridging, and who pays if it fails? How easily can one see the FX spread? How many taps to export a seed, and are you stopped by dark patterns? What is the default privacy level for sub-£50 payments? Which identity attributes are optional, and what happens if you refuse? Each answer allocates power. The screen is a mirror.

If we accept that interfaces are constitutions, we must accept constitutional duties. Publish receipts: fees broken down, spreads disclosed, paths labelled by trust assumptions. Publish rights: the right to export keys, the right to small private payments, the right to alternative relays. Publish remedies: how to appeal a freeze, how to recover from a false positive, how to escalate a dispute. Then test these in drills. Time the "withdraw all" from a custodial wallet under load. Measure confirmation variance when relays censor. Count taps to cash-out for a first-time remittance recipient in Lagos or Lahore. If the numbers shame you, the constitution needs an amendment.

There is also an ethics of absence. Some toggles should not exist. "Allow merchant to debit future payments without limit" is an invitation to abuse; if offered, it must be bound by clear caps and expiry. "Share contacts to find friends" in a wallet is a social graph extraction puncturing financial privacy; if offered, it must occur locally, not via a server that can be subpoenaed. "Enable recovery by vendor" is a delegation of sovereignty; if offered, it must be reversible without new risk. What an interface refuses to normalise is as political as what it blesses.

None of this is theoretical ornament. In minutes of stress—during a bank's weekend failure, a sanctions announcement, a local currency's overnight devaluation—the interface is the state. It either gives you a path that works or a spinner that gaslights. It either shows the fee or hides the tax. It either assumes you are competent or collapses you into a case number.

The forward test is as blunt as it is civic. If your provider must comply with a surprise freeze order, will the app say so plainly, timestamp it, and list the law—or will it display a vague error? If a regulator caps anonymous payments at £100 per day, will the wallet make the rule legible and avoid logging more than needed—or will it collect everything "just in case"? If a bridge route is risky, will the button say "high risk, centralised signers, £X cap"—or will it say "fast" with a lightning bolt? If a recovery flow shifts your trust boundary, will it ask, cleanly, "Do you consent?", with a reversible path—or will it default you into a dependency you cannot unwind?

These are not details. They are the constitution. The lines we design on glass decide, long before any courtroom, who counts and who waits. If freedom in monetary life is what survives contact, usability is the contact surface. Treat it with the seriousness of law, because that is what it quietly is.

Chapter 7
Crypto-Economics — Incentives, Games, and Adversaries

In June 2020, an anonymous developer deployed "YAM", a new DeFi token with a governance mechanism designed to rebalance supply automatically. Within thirty-six hours, the token's market value soared past $500 million. Within forty-eight, a single arithmetic bug collapsed it to near zero. No hack. No theft. Merely a mis-specified rule in a monetary game that had grown faster than its governance could think. The episode condensed the entire modern crypto-economic dilemma: wealth created by code, destroyed by code, explained by no one. Money as game theory running live.

The idea that currencies are games is not new. Every central bank operates a loop of incentives, expectations, and enforcement. What blockchain systems did was expose the machinery, remove the referees, and let the players see the scoreboard in real time. Consensus replaced authority; rewards replaced decrees. It sounded neutral. It was not. The codebase became a constitution, the miners became legislators, and the token replaced the gavel. Every parameter — block time, inflation schedule, validator penalty — became a lever of power. The rhetoric of decentralisation often hides how tightly these levers concentrate benefit. The craft of crypto-economics begins where the slogans end: designing incentives that outlast mania and resist collusion.

To understand why this matters, look beyond the charts. What distinguishes a token that sustains value from one that merely performs speculation is not hype but *work*: the capacity to link ownership to productive contribution. Productive tokens compensate those who validate, secure, or coordinate real services — blockspace, bandwidth, compute, liquidity. Narrative tokens, by contrast, derive price from expectation alone, floating on community and charisma. The boundary between them defines whether a network behaves like an economy or a casino. Supply schedules, revenue rights, and burn mechanics are not technicalities; they are moral decisions about who gains when a system grows. Design them poorly, and speculation becomes governance.

The first section of this chapter dissects that frontier. It traces how credible token design demands separability — between speculation and service, between reward and rent. We will examine how protocols like Helium, Filecoin, and EigenLayer attempted to tie token issuance to external utility, and what each revealed about the fragility of "productive" claims. We will also map the mechanics that signal sincerity: capped supply linked to real revenue, transparent emission schedules, redeemable utility. Tokens should function less like chips at a casino table and more like shares in a co-operative that actually does work.

But incentives never operate in isolation. They run through games — literal ones, coded into every block proposal and auction. The pursuit of fairness here is not aesthetic; it is existential. Miner Extractable Value (MEV) — the profit miners or validators can capture by reordering, censoring, or inserting transactions — exemplifies this tension. In January 2023, a single Ethereum validator extracted over $200,000 in arbitrage from a sandwich attack that disadvantaged retail users. MEV is not a bug; it is market structure meeting permissionless transparency. Attempts to curb it — Flashbots' "MEV-Boost", for example — introduce their own power asymmetries, effectively creating "trusted relays" that decide which transactions see daylight first. Neutrality is engineered, but never free. The cost is centralisation.

This chapter's second section addresses that cost head-on. It will interrogate the claims of anti-MEV systems — fair ordering protocols, encrypted mempools, auction-based sequencing — and propose clear criteria to evaluate them: transparency, liveness, and replayability. Each mechanism trades efficiency for justice, speed for impartiality. The recurring question is whether fairness can be credibly automated or whether it must remain a social contract above the code. The same algorithms that prevent collusion can, under different incentives, entrench it.

Beyond single chains lies the new empire of risk: bridges. They promise interoperability — seamless movement of value across ecosystems — but deliver exposure on a planetary scale. In February 2022, the Wormhole bridge was hacked for $320 million; the hole was patched by a corporate backer with deep pockets, not by decentralised consensus. In March 2022, the Ronin bridge linked to Axie Infinity lost $625 million to attackers traced to North Korea. These were not small flaws; they were the direct consequence of economic architecture. Bridges concentrate assets from multiple chains into single vaults guarded by minimal multisigs. The convenience is immense. So is the blast radius. Cross-chain coordination creates cross-chain contagion. The next part of this chapter asks what "credible neutrality" means when risk itself becomes systemic — and whether real interoperability requires less connectivity, not more.

Where bridges expose technical fragility, treasuries expose political fragility. Every ecosystem that survives long enough accumulates a treasury: a collective budget denominated in its own token. These funds pay developers, market makers, researchers, and lobbyists. They also create factions, gatekeeping, and soft patronage. The DAO that disperses grants becomes the ministry that sets orthodoxy. The longer the budget lasts, the thicker the bureaucracy grows. In late 2021, several Layer-2 networks found themselves quietly bankrolling the same handful of foundations and consultancies — firms that spoke the language of decentralisation while operating as unelected ministries. Money, even when minted from thin air, reproduces hierarchy. The final section of this chapter explores how to measure and counter that capture: transparent grant accounting, time-limited budgets, rotating councils, and public disclosure of conflicts. Governance, in short, must cost something to the governors.

Threaded through all these domains — tokens, fairness, bridges, and treasuries — is a single question: *what does it take to make coordination honest when everyone has something to gain by cheating?* The answer will not be found in mathematics alone. Crypto-economics is less a subfield of cryptography than a reassertion of political economy under new constraints: where code is constitution, liquidity is legislature, and adversaries are domestic, not foreign. Every system must assume bad faith and yet remain functional. Every protocol must quantify temptation and then price it away. The enemy is not malice but misaligned incentive.

The chapter's motif is the *game board*. Every piece on it — token, validator, bridge, DAO, relay — moves under rules that someone wrote and everyone interprets. Some squares reward work; others reward speculation. Some moves strengthen the commons; others drain it. The art is in designing a board that remains playable when stakes rise and when players conspire. Game theory was once an academic pursuit; now it is infrastructure. Crypto-economics turns it into civil engineering.

As the reader proceeds, expect no morality tales of heroes or villains. Expect mechanics, evidence, and trade-offs. We will ask why neutrality requires cost, why fairness demands transparency, why bridges that promise openness often create empires, and why treasuries built for collective good so often drift into oligarchy. What ties them together is the discipline of incentive design — the recognition that in programmable economies, freedom and exploitation are separated only by one line of code and one misplaced assumption about human nature.

The payoff of this chapter is not cynicism but clarity. Once you see that every "tokenomics" chart is a political document, every "fair ordering" system a moral choice, every "bridge" a security treaty, and every "grant" a campaign budget, you can begin to design systems that trade less on faith and more on alignment. The game will not end. But it can, with discipline, be made fairer.

Token Design Beyond Speculation

On 12 August 2020, the decentralised wireless network Helium announced that over 10,000 hotspots had been deployed worldwide. The project's token, HNT, had surged nearly 300 per cent in a month. By the following summer, venture capital poured in, coverage maps expanded, and the token's market capitalisation briefly crossed $5 billion. Yet in 2022, *Forbes* revealed that the majority of Helium's revenue—less than $6,500 a month—came not from customers using the network, but from participants mining tokens to sell to one another. A currency meant to reward a real-world service had devolved into a self-referential game. The network functioned technically, but economically it was hollow. The code worked; the incentives didn't.

This tension—between productive and narrative tokens—sits at the centre of every crypto-economic design. It defines whether a token system sustains real work or merely narrates it. *Productive tokens* are backed by measurable service: computation, storage, bandwidth, credit provision, or security. Their supply schedules, rights, and cashflows link to economic activity. *Narrative tokens* depend on belief: future adoption, community identity, or abstract promises of "governance". Both can create wealth; only one creates lasting value. The distinction is not moral, but structural. Where productive tokens bind to work, narrative tokens bind to words.

The motif here is the *link*—the invisible tether between token and task. Break that link, and speculation rushes in to fill the void. Maintain it, and speculation becomes a funding mechanism for useful coordination. The challenge is to design systems whose incentives survive tranquillity as well as mania, where the link between code and cashflow remains taut.

The modern experiment in tokenised coordination began in 2017 with the first wave of Initial Coin Offerings (ICOs). Projects such as Bancor, Tezos, and Filecoin raised hundreds of millions on the promise that tokens would align networks around shared goals. Most did not. Bancor's BNT token promised "liquidity through mathematics", yet its price detached from its underlying use within months. Filecoin, by contrast, spent years building the infrastructure that linked its token to decentralised storage capacity, launching its mainnet in October 2020 with a model that paid miners only when data was proven to be stored. Show → Name → Explain → Implication: Filecoin demonstrated that credible supply discipline and verifiable work anchors value. Bancor showed that algorithmic curiosity, without use, floats into narrative.

A productive token, then, must express three properties: *bounded issuance*, *defined rights*, and *observable revenue*. Bounded issuance keeps dilution predictable; defined rights specify what the holder can do beyond resale; observable revenue makes the token's economics falsifiable. Ethereum's post-merge shift to a burn mechanism tied to transaction fees exemplifies this triad. Supply growth fell near zero; validators earn rewards for staking; fees link to actual network use. The implication is profound: the protocol now behaves like a business with revenue and dividends, not a perpetual motion machine fuelled by narrative. It accrues value because it burns value.

Contrast this with "governance tokens" that proliferated across DeFi during 2021. Uniswap's UNI, Compound's COMP, and SushiSwap's SUSHI distributed tokens with voting rights but no intrinsic claim on revenue. Their holders could propose fee switches or policy changes but had no guaranteed cashflows. The price of participation became the price of belief. Governance, untethered from obligation, became theatre. When Uniswap later considered activating protocol fees to direct revenue to tokenholders, it confronted the legal and philosophical paradox of many decentralised projects: to create productive value may invite regulatory classification as a security; to avoid it means living forever in the narrative economy. The implication is not that one path is right, but that speculation is the tax paid for ambiguity.

Metrics expose the difference. In 2021, Uniswap processed roughly $1 trillion in trading volume, generating over $1 billion in fees, yet none flowed to tokenholders. By comparison, Lido's stETH token, representing staked Ethereum, accrued tangible yield—derived from network rewards—shared with holders. One design binds token value to operational performance; the other binds it to sentiment. In economic terms, productive tokens internalise value creation; narrative tokens externalise it into discourse.

Helium's cautionary tale reappears here. Its token model rewarded hardware deployment before verifying network demand. Tokens poured into the hands of early adopters, not customers. When actual usage lagged, the link between supply and revenue snapped. This is the recurring hazard of "bootstrapping by issuance": inflation-funded incentives can seed participation, but unless they decay into a sustainable fee economy, they become Ponzi feedback loops. Every project that prints tokens to attract users faces this cliff. The metric to watch is not price, but the share of income derived from non-token activity. In Helium's case, that ratio stayed near zero. In Filecoin's, it slowly rose.

The next design question is how to embed rights. A token's legal fiction—utility, governance, yield-bearing instrument—is irrelevant to its economic truth. What matters is what holders can enforce. Do they have the right to redeem, to vote, to receive revenue, to migrate? Bitcoin holders have the right to transact freely under consensus rules, but no claim on protocol revenue. That purity is why Bitcoin remains speculation-proof: its value derives from finality, not yield. Most other projects attempt to hybridise, granting governance influence or staking returns. The danger is subtle capture. Governance concentrated in token whales, or staking yields funded by emissions rather than fees, disguise centralisation behind community rhetoric. Productive tokens must resist the temptation to monetise governance itself. Power, once priced, tends to consolidate.

One counter-example deserves credit. MakerDAO's DAI stablecoin binds issuance to over-collateralised loans; its governance token, MKR, absorbs residual risk and can be diluted to recapitalise the system. In June 2022, when crypto markets plunged and liquidations surged, the mechanism worked as intended. DAI maintained its peg because risk had a buyer. MKR holders bore it. This is productive tokenomics in miniature: clearly defined work (collateral management), visible revenue (stability fees), and transparent downside (dilution). The lesson is not that every project should mimic Maker, but that credible design requires explicit risk assignment. Narrative tokens celebrate upside; productive tokens survive losses.

Speculation itself is not the enemy. It is the energy that finances frontier building. The question is how to direct it. A token that can only rise attracts gamblers; one that pays for honest labour attracts builders. The art lies in *programming deflation into narrative*. Supply discipline—the willingness to remove issuance when unearned—serves as a moral signal. When Ethereum's EIP-1559 began burning base fees in August 2021, it imposed cost on every transaction, aligning network use with scarcity. The system became self-pruning. That design, not its marketing, built confidence.

A credible counter-argument insists that even narrative tokens create value through coordination. Communities such as Dogecoin or Shiba Inu, while devoid of underlying cashflows, achieved durable cultural power. Their holders became marketers, meme-makers, fundraisers for charities and sponsorships. In effect, the narrative itself became the productive asset: attention. But the volatility of attention is the volatility of value. When memes fatigue, liquidity dies. The reconciliation is that "productive" can mean more than material work—it can mean durable coordination—but it must remain measurable. Attention economies need metrics beyond price: sustained activity, transaction throughput, contribution diversity. Otherwise, the story loops endlessly into itself.

The broader implication is that token design is political economy coded into incentives. Supply determines who benefits from growth; rights determine who governs; revenue links determine who sustains. Each decision redistributes power across time. Over-issuance rewards insiders now; real yield rewards users later. Hidden inflation launders control; transparent burns decentralise it. The test of maturity for any protocol is whether its token can survive low prices and low attention. A design that only works during mania is a design that has already failed.

The *link* motif returns here. Imagine every token tied by a cable to a real metric: transactions processed, storage provided, computation executed, bandwidth relayed. As long as the cable stays taut, value flows. When it slackens, noise floods in. The work of crypto-economics is to keep the link under tension—elastic enough to grow, firm enough to resist narrative drift. It requires governance with teeth, accounting with honesty, and issuance schedules that treat dilution as debt, not generosity.

The forward test is unforgiving. If all token incentives vanished tomorrow, what would remain? Would the system still perform useful work, process meaningful activity, attract genuine users? If not, the token is the product, not the fuel. The real measure of design is not capitalisation, but substitution: if speculation leaves, does the system keep running? Productive tokens answer yes, because they encode service into value. Narrative tokens answer maybe, because they encode faith into price. The difference is the link—and whether we remember to keep it fastened.

MEV, Collusion, and Credible Fairness

At 07:43 UTC on 15 September 2022, Ethereum's "Merge" finalised. Proof-of-work stopped; proof-of-stake began. Within minutes, most blocks flowed through third-party relays implementing MEV-Boost, a marketplace designed by Flashbots to auction blockspace to specialised builders. The aim was pragmatic: channel Miner/Maximal Extractable Value out of the dark and into a competitive, measurable process. Then a complication surfaced. In the wake of U.S. Treasury sanctions against Tornado Cash on 8 August 2022 in Washington, D.C., several popular relays filtered transactions that touched sanctioned contracts. Blocks still arrived. Some transactions didn't. A new paradox stood in the light: to reduce extractive behaviour, the network had concentrated power at chokepoints that could be leaned on by policy. Fairness is never free.

The problem of MEV sounds clinical. It is visceral. The order of a queue can decide who pays rent, who eats slippage, who is censored. The queue decides value. In transparent ledgers with programmable money, transaction ordering is a scarce resource. Whoever controls it can skim arbitrage ("sandwiches"), insert liquidations, or withhold competitors' trades. That power attracts collusion. Neutrality must be engineered—and paid for. The guiding motif here is the *queue.* Who lines up where, who moves to the front, and who controls the turnstile.

Show → Name → Explain → Implication. Start with the show: MEV-Boost. Name the actors: proposers, builders, relays, and searchers. Explain the machinery: validators outsource block construction to a market of builders, who assemble bundles of transactions, extract profits from ordering, and bid to have their blocks proposed. Relays broker this exchange, providing a trusted handoff so proposers see bids without seeing contents until they commit. Implication: value that miners once captured informally and opaquely becomes explicit revenue in an auction. But the relay becomes a gate. Gates can be captured.

A second show: Solana's Jito auctions. In 2023, the Jito client introduced block-engineering features and auctions for top-of-block access, seeking to reduce spam and allocate ordering rights transparently. Name the trade: by formalising access, networks can meter spam and return revenue to validators and (indirectly) stakers. Explain the catch: any centralised auction house or dominant client risks cartel dynamics. If a few builders and relays capture most flow, they set de facto rules and rents. Implication: solving for visible fairness can entrench invisible oligopoly.

What, precisely, should we call "MEV"? It is not merely bad actors ambushing retail. It is any profit available from reordering, inserting, or censoring transactions beyond their bare inclusion. Triangular arbitrage, cross-DEX price alignment, and liquidation keepers often stabilise markets; "sandwiching" and griefing do not. Neutrality is not the absence of extraction. It is credible rules for *who may* extract *what*, at *what price*, and *to whose benefit*. That requires criteria. It also requires courage to accept cost.

Three criteria judge anti-MEV claims: *transparency, liveness, and composability*. Transparency asks: can outsiders inspect who won, what they paid, and how surplus was split among builders, proposers, and—ideally—users? Liveness asks: does the system include honest transactions promptly even when builders disagree or relays fail? Composability asks: do anti-MEV measures break contracts' ability to interact predictably, or do they preserve the Lego-like property that makes programmable finance powerful? Any design that scores well on all three will still face trade-offs in latency and overhead. But the scores let us compare claims with courage, not vibes.

Consider transparency. When MEV-Boost launched, Flashbots published data pipelines and research dashboards. Builders competed on price; researchers traced revenue. That public accounting was a step forward from purely private ordering on single exchanges. Yet the same relay model that allowed audit also allowed soft censorship: compliant relays could exclude disfavoured flows, and their dominance made inclusion variance a political variable. The credible fix is plurality. Relays must be many, open-source, geographically diverse, and easy to swap. Builders must face low barriers to entry. Proposers must be able to fall back to local construction when relays misbehave. No single turnstile should decide the queue.

Now liveness. A fair ordering scheme that stalls is theatre. Designs such as encrypted mempools (e.g., Shutter's approach on Ethereum) propose to hide transaction contents until ordering is fixed. That blunts sandwiching but introduces new failure modes: decryption key delays, single points of failure in key distribution, and coordination griefing. If a malicious actor withholds keys, the block misses or transactions roll. Liveness drops. The engineering response is redundancy and slashing—multiple key providers, time-bound decryptions, and penalties for non-disclosure. Again, the cost is real: additional latency, extra infrastructure, more surface area.

Then composability. Fair-ordering protocols like "first-come-first-served with cryptographic attestations" promise less manipulation but can clash with smart-contract patterns that assume mempool preview and atomic arbitrage. If price discovery slows, spreads widen; if bundles cannot express dependencies, protocols that rely on atomic liquidations break. A credible design minimises contract-level breakage or clearly signals new assumptions so that developers can adapt. Neutrality that freezes innovation is not neutral. It is bias toward incumbents with patience.

A common counter-argument insists that MEV is *good* when left to markets. Let searchers compete; let the highest bidder win; let users pay via tips if they care. This argument carries weight in high-liquidity contexts where arbitrage tightens prices and liquidations cleanse risk. But it fails for two reasons. First, *search costs* are not symmetric. Retail users cannot bid competitively for protection. Second, *externalities* are real: sandwiching imposes hidden taxes on ordinary trades, and latency games (spam, backrunning) degrade network health. The reconciliation is to *meter* MEV—permit the forms that stabilise markets while taxing or banning the predatory kinds. That requires governance, not slogans.

What would "credible fairness" look like in practice? It would express four behaviours observable by any motivated outsider. First, *surplus sharing*: do users or protocols receive rebates when their flow is used to generate MEV? Several experiments route a portion of extracted value to LPs or protocol treasuries. Second, *predictable inclusion*: if a transaction meets fee and validity rules, it lands within a bounded time across all major relays. Third, *open auction rules*: builders and proposers compete on clear, auditable criteria; preferential access is minimised. Fourth, *exit paths*: if a relay censors or stalls, proposers can bypass it quickly without losing expected revenue. Measure these behaviours; then rank designs.

The role of "enshrined PBS" (proposer-builder separation inside the protocol) sits at the centre of ongoing debates. Moving what Flashbots pioneered off-chain into consensus logic could reduce trust in relays and formalise auctions. Yet enshrinement is not a spell. It must choose defaults: who runs the auction, how bids flow, how to resist cancelling at the last moment ("time-bandit" issues), and how to limit out-of-protocol collusion. Enshrinement shifts discretion from private actors to protocol rules. It doesn't remove it. Strong rules still cost latency, code complexity, and social coordination for upgrades. But they also deny a few firms the ability to define fairness by interface.

Two named, checkable episodes sharpen the stakes. In March 2022, a widely discussed "sandwich" accounted for six-figure profit routed through a single builder on Ethereum in one interval—an event dissected in public dashboards and research notes. The forensic detail made something clear: measurable MEV attracts sophisticated capital, which gravitates to a small number of professional builders with privileged connectivity. Concentration followed transparency. In April 2023, Solana core devs and the Jito team coordinated on making block auctions and "quic" networking improvements reduce spam and failed transactions during hotspots of meme-coin trading. Inclusion rates improved; fee markets stabilised locally. But some validators defaulted to clients that privileged particular auction flows, raising concerns about client monoculture. Each fix revealed a fresh fault line.

The cleanest counter-example to MEV pessimism comes from domains where ordering has been engineered successfully without authoritarian control: financial exchanges with frequent batch auctions (FBA) and minimal information leakage. Designs that clear all bids and asks in discrete intervals reduce sniping and enforce fair price. Several crypto projects have prototyped FBA-like mechanisms. The limitation is obvious. Batch auctions add delay; they change the feel of "real-time" finance; they can complicate composability across protocols expecting continuous time. Still, they demonstrate that fairness can be *priced* rather than *preached.*

We should also separate "anti-MEV" theatre from substance. A wallet that claims to protect users by "private orderflow" but routes it exclusively to a single builder has solved nothing; it has merely sold flow. A relay that calls itself neutral but filters by jurisdictional risk is not neutral; it is lawful and centralised. A chain that markets "MEV-resistance" but lacks public metrics on inclusion variance and builder concentration has not earned trust. Credible fairness is an audit trail, not a tagline.

If the queue is the motif, the user's vantage is the test. What should a citizen of a monetary network demand to see? Three receipts. One that shows *who* sequenced their transaction and *why* it took the slot it did; one that itemises *what* they paid—base fee, tip, any auction rebate; and one that states *where* their flow travelled—public mempool, encrypted channel, direct to builder. If a provider cannot furnish these receipts, the neutrality they promise is unverifiable.

Of course, neutrality itself is a political claim. Censorship resistance and credible inclusion become incompatible at the extremes. If you require universal inclusion, you must punish relays that differ; if you tolerate variance, you must accept that some relays will filter. The only coherent stance is pluralism with escape: multiple relays, multiple clients, clear fallbacks, and social norms that punish captured behaviour by routing around it. Diversity is not decoration. It is the only defence against cartel logic.

Costs remain. More relays mean more coordination. Encrypted channels mean more complexity. Batch auctions mean more latency. Sharing surplus means thinner margins for validators. The temptation will be to cheat the hard parts—return to private mempools, privileged pipes, and soft promises. Resist that. Pay the cost where it does the least harm: a few dozen extra milliseconds rather than a single firm owning your flow, a slightly smaller validator yield rather than a tax on every retail trade; a visible delay in exchange for predictable inclusion. Price fairness honestly.

The forward test is crisp. If a single relay fails tonight, will transactions still land within bound? If a jurisdiction leans on builders, can proposers switch lanes without re-writing their stack? If a wallet promises protection, can an independent researcher validate that protection across a month of data? If not, the queue belongs to someone else. Engineer neutrality at cost, or accept collusion at discount. Those are the only two prices on the board.

Bridges and the Empire of Risk

On 23 March 2022 in Ho Chi Minh City, Sky Mavis—the company behind Axie Infinity—disclosed that the Ronin bridge had been drained of crypto-assets worth roughly $625 million. Weeks later, the FBI (April 2022) attributed the operation to North Korea's Lazarus Group. The sequence was brutally simple: compromise a small set of validators, authorise fake withdrawals, and walk value off one chain and on to another before alarms converged. The bridge failed. Funds vanished. The fuse burned all the way through.

Cross-chain bridges promise the internet's old miracle—*anywhere to anywhere*—for value. They turn islands of computation into bustling archipelagos. They also centralise peril. A bridge commonly escrows assets on Chain A and issues a promise on Chain B. If the escrow is forged or the promise is mis-issued, the accounting unravels everywhere at once. Chainalysis (August 2022) estimated that over $2 billion had been stolen from bridges that year alone. The message, repeated across audits and post-mortems, is not subtle: convenience compounds risk. Each new corridor concentrates more travellers, more tolls, and more targets. The fuse gets shorter.

Show → Name → Explain → Implication. Start with the show. In February 2022, the Wormhole bridge connecting Solana and Ethereum suffered an exploit of about $320 million. Jump Crypto publicly committed to backstop the loss, restoring solvency within days. Name the design: lock-and-mint, mediated by guardians who attest that funds were locked on one side so that a wrapped asset could be minted on the other. Explain the failure: signature verification bypass let an attacker mint without locking. Implication: when a single gateway confers minting power, all downstream "assets" depend on that gate's integrity and its sponsor's balance sheet.

A second show. In June 2022, Harmony's Horizon bridge was hacked for around $100 million, again traced by multiple analytics firms to North Korean actors. Name the pattern: a small, permissioned multisig. Explain: five signers, two keys compromised, threshold met, vault open. Implication: if a national-level adversary only needs to subvert a handful of keys, the bridge is not a bridge. It is a vault door with loose hinges.

What, then, is a bridge? Three archetypes matter. *Lock-and-mint* (the most common): assets are locked on Chain A; a claim is minted on Chain B. *Burn-and-release*: the claim on B is burned; the lock on A is released. *Light-client verification*: Chain B runs a verifier for Chain A's consensus so it can check proofs of events without trusting a committee. The third is stronger in principle because it reduces trust to cryptography and liveness, but it is costlier in verification and engineering. Most deployed bridges still rely on committees, relays, or oracles. The convenience is obvious. So is the blast radius.

The motif for this subchapter is the *fuse*. Bridges are fuses—thin links that carry enormous load until they fail, at which point they decide how much of the circuit they protect and how much they burn. Short, cheap, and hot fuses abound: multisigs, trusted relays, custodial wrappers. Long, cool, expensive fuses exist too: light-clients, optimistic verification with fraud proofs, staggered withdrawals. The design question is not whether to have a fuse. It is where to place it, how thick to make it, and who pays when it blows.

Bridge risk is not abstract. It shows up in behaviours and metrics. *Concentration*: two or three bridges often hold the majority of a chain's external value; a single exploit becomes systemic. *Signer entropy*: if keys cluster within one firm or jurisdiction, legal and operational capture become single-points of failure. *Withdrawal latency*: instant redemptions feel humane but remove time to detect fraud; enforced delays buy safety at the price of UX. *Circuit breakers*: caps per asset and per epoch temper contagion; most don't exist until after a disaster. Measure these, and rhetoric gives way to governance.

Ronin and Wormhole were not anomalies; Nomad (August 2022) lost about $190 million to a "copy-paste" vulnerability that let anyone replay a "valid" message once the initial exploit showed the way. The queue turned into loot. The pattern was collective rather than adversarial: hundreds of opportunists drained funds in public, some later returning them. It was a stress test on social capital, not just code. Bridges are not only technical artefacts; they are institutions that must survive *multiple* classes of adversary—state actors, professional thieves, and panicked crowds.

A credible counter-example tempers fatalism. The Cosmos ecosystem's Inter-Blockchain Communication (IBC) protocol uses light-client verification to authenticate cross-chain messages. Rather than trusting a committee, chains verify each other's headers and proofs. Similarly, within Polkadot's architecture, messages pass through a shared security layer with defined guarantees. These designs reduce the trust surface dramatically. They also impose costs: engineering complexity, heavier proof systems, and limitations on which chains can interoperate easily. The reconciliation is honest: stronger fuses cost throughput and flexibility. They still blow, but they are designed to do so without torching the house.

Economics deepens the trap. Bridges thrive on *Total Value Locked.* More value attracts better market makers, which attracts more users, which attracts more value. The same flywheel magnifies downside: the larger the honeypot, the more capital a sophisticated adversary will deploy to study, infiltrate, and capture it. There is also fee gravity: routing front-ends default to the cheapest, fastest path; cheap, fast bridges become de facto standards, regardless of their trust assumptions. A metric to watch is the spread between a bridge's fees and the implied cost of its security assumptions. When that spread looks too good to be true, it is pricing in *your* risk as its buffer.

Bridge risk is not purely cryptographic. In mid-2023, the Multichain service collapsed into confusion after reported arrests of key personnel in China; funds became stranded; governance communications fractured. No exploit was necessary. A human chokepoint jammed the fuse. That episode exposed an under-discussed variable: *operator opacity*. If a bridge's control plane relies on a few people, a single jurisdiction, or private servers, then *law*, not code, is the attack surface. The implication is constitutional: cross-chain finance cannot outrun off-chain governance indefinitely.

Designers often answer with "optimistic" bridges—assume messages are honest, give a fraud window for watchers to contest. This lowers immediate cost and broadens compatibility, but it shifts burden to monitoring. Who pays watchers? What penalties exist for missing fraud? How many independent watchers exist, and where are they domiciled? Without funded adversaries on the honest side, the optimism is naïve. An optimistic system needs a cynical budget.

Pair abstractions with decisions. *Trust* is not a slogan; it is whether a user will route a life's savings through a contract whose signers they cannot name. *Efficiency* is not a boast; it is the median time-to-finality across a week of usage without failed redeems. *Risk* is not a mood; it is the ex-ante loss if the largest signer becomes malicious—valued in basis points of TVL—and the ex-post time to halt and unwind when alarms trip. If those numbers are unknown, the bridge is running on wish.

Engineers reach for mitigations. Some add *rate limiters* to slow redemptions when anomalies appear. Some diversify *signer sets* across hardware enclaves, geographies, and firms. Some publish *proofs of reserves* for wrapped assets with independent attestations. These help. They do not change the empire logic: each new route adds another customs gate; each customs gate accumulates discretion; discretion accumulates rents. A bridge that becomes an *ecosystem's* default is not a protocol; it is a central bank without a charter.

Two named, checkable examples illustrate how convenience rewrites governance. First, after the Wormhole exploit, Jump's backstop prevented broad contagion. That private bailout created a precedent: systemic bridges may become "too big to fail" and rely on corporate treasuries to socialise risk implicitly. Second, after the Ronin hack, Sky Mavis increased validator count and distribution, added external validators, and imposed new procedures. Security improved; the core team remained the fulcrum. Both outcomes reflect the same truth: failure triggers centralisation, not the reverse. The fuse is replaced with a thicker, more expensive one tied to fewer hands.

A frequent objection asserts that *the future is cross-chain*: user demand compels easy movement; composability across ecosystems is the point. There is merit here. Liquidity wants to flow where it earns; developers want their apps to meet users *where they are*. But "cross-chain" has two meanings. One is teleportation—assets hop across security domains as if governance differences did not exist. The other is *clearing*—positions are netted across domains with final settlement channelled back to a small set of high-assurance links. The first model pretends away sovereignty; the second disciplines it. The bias of this book is clear: prefer clearing over teleportation; prefer narrow, strong fuses over broad, brittle ones.

What, then, should evaluators demand from bridges before they trust them with scale? Four behaviours, each testable. *Caps*: hard per-asset and per-epoch limits that throttle loss. *Diversity*: signer sets that cross firms and jurisdictions, with public rotation schedules. *Liveness under failure*: documented fallbacks—light-client paths, local exits, or time-locked withdrawals—when relays stall. *Public drills*: rehearsed, timestamped incident games whose outcomes are published. If these are absent, the fuse is ornamental.

Interoperability can be *priced*. Longer withdrawal windows, periodic batch settlement, and fee rebates for slower but safer routes internalise some tail risk. Wallets can annotate routes with trust assumptions—"trusted multisig", "optimistic with 7-day window", "light-client verified"—and default novices to safer paths. Exchanges can limit listings of wrapped assets that lack strong proofs of backing. None of this is glamorous. All of it reduces empire dynamics.

The fuse motif returns to expose psychology. Users forgive slowness. They rarely forgive loss. Yet products consistently invert this preference: "fast" buttons hide long-tail peril; "safe" paths are tucked behind expert menus. The empire expands by making the risky route the easy route. It must be reversed. Safety by default, risk by explicit choice, with receipts.

A final limitation deserves clarity. Even the best light-client bridges must pick manuals for consensus upgrades and reorg handling; even the best audits cannot model all cross-protocol interactions; even the best jurisdictions can be captured. Perfection is not on offer. The task is to architect systems that fail narrowly and recover publicly. That means taking composability hunger seriously. Many of the worst losses occurred when protocols depended on bridged assets as collateral for leverage; a single faulty message cascaded into liquidations. The cure is appetite control. Do not let wrapped claims become foundational money in foreign lands unless you are willing to be governed by a foreign fuse.

The forward test is blunt. If the dominant bridge in your ecosystem is halted tonight, how much value is stranded, for how long, and with what recourse? If a major jurisdiction compels signers to freeze redemptions, can funds still reach safety via an alternative path without bankrupting counterparties? If a new exploit pattern spreads across two bridges you rely on, do circuit breakers trigger by schedule or by tweet? Design for honest answers to those questions, and the empire shrinks to a federation of guarded crossings. Fail, and the next spark will find the next fuse, and the flame will travel further than you ever intended.

Treasuries, Grants, and the Political Budget

On 12 January 2021, Uniswap—the largest decentralised exchange on Ethereum—approved its first major community grant: $750,000 to fund public goods development. The decision passed with 86% support, yet nearly all the votes came from a handful of venture capital–owned wallets. The optics were uncomfortable. A project founded on decentralisation had just demonstrated how capital-weighted voting can reproduce the very hierarchies it sought to transcend. The treasury was open; the politics were not.

Every crypto ecosystem eventually meets this reckoning. Tokens may distribute ownership, but treasuries concentrate discretion. They are the fiscal arms of decentralised governance—repositories of collective value meant to fund maintenance, research, and growth. Yet each treasury also becomes a stage where influence, ideology, and inertia collide. The paradox is immediate: systems designed to reduce gatekeeping must still decide who receives grants, who sets priorities, and how much risk the community can bear. In code, all are equal; in budgets, some are more equal than others.

The motif throughout this subchapter is the *ledger as mirror*. It reflects not only transactions but values. Every disbursement encodes an implicit philosophy about fairness, legitimacy, and permanence. Who funds whom tells you who rules.

Show → Name → Explain → Implication. Consider first the show. In late 2020, the MakerDAO community voted to establish a formal *Core Unit* framework—semi-autonomous teams funded directly by the protocol's treasury. Name the actors: engineers, risk analysts, legal specialists, and governance facilitators. Explain the move: to professionalise decentralised operations without re-creating a corporation. Implication: budgets became the new code. Once a protocol can issue recurring payments, questions of employment, accountability, and political capture enter by the same door as the grants. Within months, debates over salary transparency and renewal thresholds dominated governance calls. Freedom required payroll.

Contrast that with Polkadot's *Treasury Bounty* model, introduced in 2021. Proposals are public; curators manage specific spending tracks; unused funds burn periodically. This mechanism forces velocity—money that sits idle is destroyed, incentivising active stewardship. Yet the same logic carries risk. When spending becomes mandatory to avoid waste, incentives tilt toward quantity over scrutiny. The fuse flips from inertia to indulgence. The mirror shows movement, not necessarily merit.

Treasuries are political budgets because they turn ideology into cashflow. Bitcoin avoided the problem by refusing to have one: no treasury, no formal grants, no discretionary funding. Its ecosystem relies on voluntary contributions and independent donors. That design has virtues—resilience against capture, simplicity of governance—but also clear limits. Open-source maintenance remains underfunded, and coordination relies on informal prestige rather than accountable expenditure. Ethereum's opposite path—explicit public goods funding through the Ethereum Foundation and community grants—has produced vital research but also persistent questions about soft centralisation. The foundation's discretionary power remains high, even as it funds alternatives to itself.

What distinguishes a *treasury* from a *war chest* is process. A war chest is for emergencies; a treasury is for policy. Most protocols began with the former and drifted into the latter. When token prices soared in 2021, DAO treasuries swelled into the tens of billions. Uniswap's alone exceeded $4 billion in nominal value (DeFi Pulse, November 2021). Few had procedures for budgeting, oversight, or independent audit. Governance forums turned into grant committees; debates over liquidity incentives blurred with lobbying for subsidies. The quiet creation of fiscal constitutions—who proposes, who approves, who audits—became the most consequential yet least examined layer of protocol design.

Power concentrates wherever disbursement occurs. The behaviour is measurable. Treasury proposals with high quorum thresholds correlate strongly with delegation networks: a handful of "whale" addresses effectively set agendas. Snapshot votes, though nominally open, often coincide with coordination in private Discord or Telegram groups. In 2022, researcher Kevin Owocki of Gitcoin described this dynamic as "the plutocratic trap"—wealth confers governance, governance preserves wealth. The remedy, he argued, is *plural funding*: a mixture of quadratic voting, retroactive grants, and transparent matching pools that dilute concentrated influence. The principle is sound; the practice is fraught. Retroactive funding invites selective storytelling; quadratic formulas can be gamed by sybil farms. Every algorithmic correction invents new manipulation vectors.

The counter-example lies with smaller, deliberately bounded treasuries such as Nouns DAO, launched in August 2021. Each day, one generative NFT is auctioned; proceeds fund a collective treasury managed by tokenholders. Proposals range from art installations to software grants. Governance remains simple: one Noun, one vote. The constraint is physical—only one new Noun per day—creating a slow, predictable issuance and a limited electorate. Transparency is radical; all spending is on-chain, all debate public. Yet even Nouns faces the mirror: when a handful of whales acquire hundreds of Nouns, pluralism fades. Decentralisation, like liquidity, pools.

Treasuries without disclosure are monarchies in disguise. Transparency does not end capture, but it exposes its contours. Vitalik Buterin's 2022 writings on "credible neutrality" extend naturally to finance: a treasury earns legitimacy not from decentralisation alone but from auditability and procedural clarity. The key behaviours are visible. *Proposal clarity*: plain summaries of purpose, scope, and measurable outcomes. *Disbursement transparency*: addresses, timestamps, and on-chain proofs of payment. *Post-mortem reporting*: results measured against commitments, not narratives. These are governance equivalents of financial statements. Without them, protocols drift into faith-based economics.

The *ledger as mirror* motif sharpens when grants turn political. The optimism of early DAOs presumed alignment: fund developers, grow the ecosystem, everyone wins. But every grant also privileges certain philosophies—security over experimentation, infrastructure over art, incumbents over newcomers. In late 2022, Aave's treasury funded a market-making partnership with commercial trading firms. Critics argued it contradicted the DAO's ethos of neutrality. Supporters saw it as pragmatic liquidity management. Both were right. Treasuries, like states, must balance ideals with solvency. The risk is that necessity becomes pretext for consolidation.

The data confirm a drift toward centralisation. A 2023 Electric Capital Developer Report found that fewer than 20 organisations funded more than half of all open-source commits across major crypto ecosystems. While the rhetoric is "community-led", the cheque-signing power remains concentrated. Treasury committees, grant foundations, and subDAOs operate as modern ministries—each with its own bureaucracy, alliances, and budget cycles. Capture here is quiet: not through corruption but through continuity. Those who control evaluation criteria define the future.

There are ways to measure resistance. *Turnover rate*: how frequently treasury signers, curators, or committee members rotate. *Budget diversity*: how many distinct entities receive funding per quarter. *Public challenge ratio*: how often proposals are amended or rejected after open critique. These metrics translate abstract ideals into observable governance. When all three approach zero, decentralisation is theatre.

Some communities experiment with "citizens' juries" for grants—randomly selected tokenholders voting on anonymised proposals to blunt reputational bias. Others separate financial and ideological governance, reserving one chamber for budget oversight and another for policy. These designs echo centuries of constitutional learning: separate powers, publish accounts, rotate authority. Yet each modification adds friction. Participants complain of delay; projects lobby for fast-tracks. The demand for efficiency becomes the justification for hierarchy. The empire rebuilds itself, ledger by ledger.

A credible limitation tempers cynicism. Transparency alone can't solve political bias; disclosure without literacy overwhelms. When governance dashboards flood with data but lack interpretation, power migrates to those fluent in metrics. In late 2023, several DAOs hired "transparency officers"—auditors of openness itself—who then became gatekeepers of narrative. The reconciliation is practical: transparency must be paired with intelligibility. Raw data without context creates opacity of another kind.

The fiscal sociology of DAOs has historical rhyme. In the 17th century, the Dutch East India Company pioneered shareholder governance with distributed dividends and public ledgers. Yet within decades, insider cartels dominated its board, using complex share structures to entrench control. It took parliamentary intervention to restore partial oversight. The lesson endures: financial innovation amplifies existing hierarchies unless constitutional design keeps pace. Crypto-treasuries, by echoing early joint-stock dynamics, risk re-enacting that history on-chain.

The political budget also shapes narrative. Projects that fund only developers signal a technocracy; those that fund education, art, and community signal a polis. Both are legitimate choices but must be acknowledged as such. When treasuries pretend to be apolitical, they cede definition of "value" to incumbents. The cost is cultural homogeneity. The protocols that survive will be those that understand money as speech—not in the libertarian sense of unrestrained power, but in the civic sense of accountable dialogue.

The mirror returns a final question. When you look at a protocol's ledger, what do you see? Are the disbursements diffuse, deliberate, and legible—or clustered, automatic, and opaque? Can any participant trace where collective funds go without insider knowledge? If not, decentralisation has stopped at rhetoric. The forward test is harsh but fair: if your treasury vanished tomorrow, would the community rebuild it or breathe relief? The answer reveals whether the budget served the mission—or became it.

Chapter 8
After Hegemony: Scenarios for a Multipolar Monetary Internet

In February 2022, the day Russia's tanks crossed into Ukraine, Western sanctions did something unseen in modern finance: they weaponised the infrastructure of money itself. Swift connections were cut, foreign reserves frozen, and payment rails turned from neutral plumbing into instruments of policy. Overnight, the illusion that global finance was a shared utility evaporated. Central bankers in Beijing, Delhi, and Riyadh watched closely. So did the architects of decentralised finance, who saw in the West's show of power a vindication of their own warnings: that the global monetary system, dressed as an open commons, was in fact a single-vendor network with an American root server. The question that followed was both geopolitical and technical—what comes *after* hegemony?

The monetary internet—the mesh of bank ledgers, payment processors, blockchains, and protocols that now routes nearly all human exchange—is fragmenting. What once looked like convergence now resembles *forked globalisation*: overlapping but incompatible standards, each anchored in competing sovereignties. On one side stand dollar-centric protocols, where stablecoins and correspondent banks extend U.S. jurisdiction into code. On another, central bank digital currency blocs—from China's e-CNY to pilot projects in the Gulf—offer their own managed ecosystems, built on state-level interoperability and compliance by design. Between these poles, non-aligned crypto corridors—South American remittance hubs, African fintech collectives, Asian liquidity pools—experiment with neutral settlement rails that prize access over allegiance. The result is not a single successor to dollar hegemony, but a world of overlapping monetary sovereignties, each with distinct strengths and failure modes.

Money has always been an instrument of power, but now the architecture of that power is programmable. The dollar's primacy rested on trust, liquidity, and military reach; the next order will rest on software, standards, and alliances of convenience. The struggle is already visible in code. When Circle, the issuer of USD Coin, blacklisted addresses after the Tornado Cash sanctions, it wasn't Congress that enforced policy—it was a smart contract executing a compliance call. When the People's Bank of China tested its digital yuan in Shenzhen in late 2020, it embedded state auditability at the protocol layer. In both cases, sovereignty became an API.

The *cat-and-mouse* of sanctions and compliance defines this transitional moment. Enforcement evolves through chokepoints: exchanges, stablecoin issuers, cloud providers. Counter-moves evolve through obfuscation: mixers, privacy layers, decentralised exchanges with minimal metadata. Each escalation raises costs, not only for the adversary but for ordinary users caught in the net. The more control one side asserts, the more complexity the other creates. Monetary systems become labyrinths of intent and inference—where legitimacy and opacity duel for supremacy in real time. What began as deterrence becomes drag.

Yet amid fragmentation lies an unexpected opportunity: resilience through redundancy. When no single system can be trusted universally, societies learn to build layers. A family in Lagos might hold savings in naira, transact daily through USDT on Tron, and store long-term value in Bitcoin on a hardware wallet. An NGO operating in Myanmar might mix bank transfers, crypto remittances, and offline vouchers to keep aid moving despite blockades. These aren't anomalies; they are prototypes of a more adaptive monetary ecology—one that prizes continuity over purity. A multipolar system can be chaotic, but it can also be antifragile. Diversity is defence.

Still, diversity without discipline leads to noise. Freedom, if it is to outlast fashion, must become a practice, not a posture. The coming decade will test whether users and builders can cultivate the institutional literacy to navigate multipolar finance without succumbing to chaos. That means knowing the provenance of one's assets, the custody chain of one's wallets, the jurisdictional reach of one's intermediaries. It means designing systems where exit is credible, not rhetorical—where privacy is not delusion, and usability does not mask control. Freedom becomes what survives contact with constraint.

The motif of this chapter is *practice*. Not the slogans of sovereignty, but the lived habits of resilience: layered money, distributed custody, minimal trust. These are the techniques that allow ordinary people to remain functional even as empires rearrange their protocols. If dollar hegemony taught the world dependence, its decline will teach choreography—a dance between networks rather than obedience to one.

This chapter maps that choreography. It begins by examining how the dollar's infrastructure became the substrate of globalisation, and how its own code—payment rails, correspondent banking, SWIFT, and stablecoins—now encodes both dominance and decay. It then sketches three plausible futures: the dollarised internet, the sovereign bloc, and the plural commons. Each will demand different compromises between control and autonomy. Each will generate its own politics of trust.

But more than prediction, the chapter seeks *preparation*. Monetary hegemony may fade, but monetary interdependence will not. The systems that replace it will be messy hybrids—part state, part network, part crowd. To navigate them well is to accept that freedom will not arrive as a clean break, but as a discipline: the deliberate choice to understand, diversify, and design for resilience. The age of single keys and singular powers is ending. What comes next is an era of many ledgers, many laws, and many hands—each holding, however briefly, a line of code that connects us all.

Forked Globalisation: Dollar-Centric Protocols, CBDC Blocs, and Non-Aligned Crypto Corridors Define Plausible Futures with Distinct Winners and Failure Modes

On 26 February 2022, two days after Russian forces entered Ukraine, the United States and its allies moved to disconnect several major Russian banks from the SWIFT network. Within hours, $300 billion in Russian foreign reserves—held in Western institutions—were rendered inaccessible. The seizure was silent, executed through messages and database updates rather than soldiers or seizures of gold. What the world witnessed was not a war of tanks, but of ledgers. Finance had become infrastructure, and infrastructure had become sovereign. The episode marked a hinge point: the first time a reserve currency power used the plumbing of global payments as a geopolitical weapon at scale. And with that, a decades-long assumption collapsed—the assumption that the monetary internet was neutral.

That moment clarified what many central bankers and technologists already suspected. The "global" in globalisation had always been conditional. The dollar was not merely a unit of account; it was the default operating system of world trade. Now, as nations, corporations, and networks re-examine their dependencies, that system is beginning to fork. Each fork carries its own logic, its own political grammar, and its own failure modes. The dollar still anchors the largest share of cross-border settlements—about 88% of foreign exchange turnover, according to the Bank for International Settlements (2022)—but its infrastructure is no longer uncontested. What follows is not collapse, but *pluralisation*: the emergence of parallel monetary circuits, each optimised for different forms of trust.

Show → Name → Explain → Implication. Begin with the dollar's domain. The so-called dollar-centric protocols include not only SWIFT, Fedwire, and CHIPS, but their digital extensions: dollar-backed stablecoins such as USDC, USDT, and PayPal USD. They replicate dollar hegemony in tokenised form, tethering global liquidity to American regulatory and banking systems. When Circle, the issuer of USDC, froze addresses linked to Tornado Cash in August 2022, it demonstrated that jurisdictional enforcement had become programmable. The stablecoin model amplifies the dollar's reach by making it composable within decentralised finance, yet it also inherits its choke points. One subpoena can immobilise millions of tokens; one banking disruption can ripple through entire liquidity pools. The implication is paradoxical: the more the dollar digitises, the more visible—and thus more governable—it becomes.

The alternative pole is taking shape in *CBDC blocs*. China's e-CNY pilots, launched in Shenzhen in October 2020, have already processed hundreds of billions of yuan across tens of millions of users. The architecture is explicitly hierarchical: two-tier issuance, full traceability for regulators, and partial privacy for users. It is not designed to liberate money but to domesticate it. The Digital Currency Institute of the People's Bank of China describes the goal as "controllable anonymity"—a phrase that captures the ethos of state programmable finance. Other nations are following: the European Central Bank's digital euro project, the Reserve Bank of India's wholesale trials, and the Bank of England's ongoing consultations on a "digital pound." These initiatives share a premise: sovereignty through code. Each seeks to ensure that national monetary policy and compliance frameworks survive a world of transnational platforms.

CBDC blocs do not compete only on technology. They compete on governance models. In the Chinese configuration, final settlement occurs within a closed administrative network; cross-border usage requires bilateral agreements. The European model, by contrast, aims to interoperate with existing payment rails and preserve privacy through selective disclosure. The distinction matters. A CBDC designed for surveillance will be efficient at control but fragile in legitimacy; a CBDC designed for privacy will be credible to citizens but less responsive to geopolitical enforcement. Both invite imitation. The fork is ideological as much as infrastructural: *should money serve the state, or should the state serve money's users?*

Between these poles stretches the unaligned frontier—*crypto corridors* that neither depend on the dollar nor trust official digital currencies. They are emerging where monetary sovereignty is weakest: in remittance-heavy economies such as Nigeria, Argentina, and the Philippines. In Lagos, peer-to-peer USDT transfers via the Tron network now move more value weekly than traditional bank remittances, according to Chainalysis (2023). In Buenos Aires, small businesses invoice in DAI or USDC to hedge against triple-digit inflation. These corridors treat blockchain not as ideology but as survival infrastructure. Their users may not speak of decentralisation, but they practice it daily: splitting custody across wallets, timing conversions to escape volatility, and arbitraging between regulatory zones. The unaligned bloc's advantage is agility; its weakness is stability. Without legal recognition or clear recourse, every transaction is an act of faith.

A credible counter-example complicates the picture. El Salvador's 2021 adoption of Bitcoin as legal tender was intended to leapfrog dependence on the dollar and remittance intermediaries. Two years later, usage remained limited, with most citizens preferring cash or dollars. The government's Chivo wallet faced technical issues and public mistrust. The lesson is not that crypto cannot scale, but that national adoption without institutional literacy creates fragility. Freedom needs infrastructure, but also habits. The reconciliation is subtle: decentralisation works bottom-up, not top-down. The most resilient crypto corridors are those that emerged organically—Kenya's informal stablecoin merchants, Venezuela's freelancer networks, Turkey's arbitrage traders—not those legislated into being.

The quiet motif of this section is *gravity*. Monetary gravity pulls actors toward liquidity, convenience, and credibility. The dollar's gravity persists because its markets remain deepest and its enforcement most predictable. CBDCs seek to create regional gravities—anchors for settlement within political blocs. Crypto corridors operate in microgravity, free-floating until they find or build their own centres of mass. The future of globalisation will be decided by where that gravity stabilises.

Each architecture—dollar, CBDC, or crypto—carries distinct failure modes. Dollar-centric protocols risk overreach: every act of enforcement strengthens the incentive for alternatives. A CBDC bloc risks enclosure: tight control breeds innovation flight and parallel economies. Crypto corridors risk entropy: without shared standards, interoperability devolves into fragmentation and scams. The policy temptation is to pick a winner. The wiser course is to recognise their interdependence. A multipolar monetary internet will resemble a power grid more than a hierarchy—redundant, messy, but resilient.

The data already suggest such hybridity. In 2023, the Bank for International Settlements reported that over 90% of central banks were exploring digital currencies, while global stablecoin transaction volumes surpassed $7 trillion. Meanwhile, Bitcoin's Lightning Network quietly expanded its cross-border payment capacity, providing the connective tissue between otherwise siloed systems.

The technical outcome is *layered globalisation*: settlement and liquidity distributed across overlapping domains, each enforcing its own logic of trust. The political outcome is harder to map. Who arbitrates disputes when jurisdictions overlap? Who guarantees redemption when stablecoins fail? Who bears liability when CBDC networks interoperate? These questions will define the next monetary order as much as exchange rates or trade balances once did.

To understand the forked world, follow the behaviour of institutions rather than rhetoric. The IMF now studies stablecoin governance; the Bank for International Settlements experiments with "mBridge," a cross-border CBDC corridor linking Hong Kong, Thailand, and the UAE; and major banks quietly hold stablecoins for settlement trials. Simultaneously, decentralised protocols such as Thorchain and Cosmos IBC attempt to bridge tokens without intermediaries. The boundary between formal and informal, regulated and autonomous, is dissolving. Globalisation continues, but under multiple rulesets.

The deeper implication concerns *trust*. The post-Bretton Woods order rested on the promise that dollars anywhere were as good as dollars at home. The forked order replaces that singular promise with a spectrum of assurances. Some will be legal—redeemable by law. Others will be cryptographic—verifiable by code. Others still will be social—backed by reputation and use. Each user, firm, or nation must decide which layer to trust and when to switch. The future of globalisation is not one network but many crossings.

The motif of gravity returns in the closing movement. Empires rarely end with collapse; they decay into constellations. The dollar's orbit will remain vast, but its pull will no longer be absolute. The e-CNY and digital euro will anchor regional ecosystems. Non-aligned crypto corridors will route around both, weaving liquidity through informal exchanges and remittance rails. Between them, new intermediaries—wallet providers, bridges, compliance oracles—will rise as the diplomats of the monetary internet. Their allegiances will be fluid, their incentives hybrid.

The forward test, then, is stark. When a payment fails across borders in 2030, which support desk will you call? When a nation sanctions an address, which ledger will obey? When inflation erodes a domestic unit, which alternative will citizens choose instinctively? These questions are not speculative. They are already being answered transaction by transaction, protocol by protocol. Forked globalisation is not a forecast. It is the operating condition of the century's second monetary network. The only uncertainty is whose gravity will hold longest before the next fork begins.

Sanctions, Compliance, and the Cat-and-Mouse

On 8 August 2022 in Washington, D.C., the U.S. Treasury's Office of Foreign Assets Control sanctioned the Tornado Cash smart contracts. Within a day, Circle froze USDC at flagged addresses; major interfaces geofenced access; relay operators in Ethereum's post-Merge stack began filtering transactions that touched the sanctioned code. No courtroom. No handcuffs. A policy memo had changed the topology of a network. The chokepoint moved to code.

That episode distilled the modern sanctions playbook: shift enforcement from borders to *chokepoints*—issuers, relays, custodians, cloud providers—then amplify surveillance until private acts become public signals. The response was equally modern. Users routed through non-censoring infrastructure; developers forked interfaces; privacy advocates pointed to humanitarian costs when whole classes of transactions slowed or failed. Each move carried a price. Enforcement raised compliance overhead and technical debt; evasion raised latency, fees, and legal risk. The cat-and-mouse had entered the mempool.

Show → Name → Explain → Implication. Begin with *surveillance.* Blockchain analysis firms—Chainalysis, Elliptic, TRM Labs—convert public ledgers into risk maps. They cluster addresses, score flows, and flag suspicious patterns for exchanges and banks. This is not speculative capability. In February 2022 in New York, U.S. authorities arrested two individuals accused of laundering funds from the 2016 Bitfinex hack after tracing layer upon layer of transactions and decrypting cloud-stored keys. The behaviour was visible: seemingly unrelated wallets converged; redemptions brushed KYC perimeters; metadata leaked. The implication is stark. Public ledgers collapse time. They grant investigators leverage that used to require subpoenas across continents.

Next, *chokepoints*. In February 2022, after Russia's invasion of Ukraine, several Russian banks were cut off from SWIFT; by late February and March, foreign exchange reserves were partially immobilised in Western institutions. The show was global settlement turning selective overnight. Name the reality: payment messaging, correspondent banking, and reserve custody—each a valve with an address. Explain the technique: freeze at the hub, starve the spokes. Implication: systems designed for efficiency double as levers of power. The more centralised the rail, the easier the pull.

A subtler chokepoint emerged after Ethereum's Merge on 15 September 2022. Validators began outsourcing block building to third-party relays via MEV-Boost. Some relays—citing legal risk post-Tornado sanctions—filtered transactions touching flagged contracts. Blocks still arrived; certain users waited. The abstraction "censorship" translated into a behaviour: inclusion variance. A transaction valid by consensus rules could take longer or fail if it brushed the wrong cluster. The implication: neutrality cannot be assumed from base-layer rules if infrastructure operators can be pressured. The chokepoint is any switch you cannot route around.

Enforcement, however, is never omnipotent. The first credible counter-example is practical: *humanitarian carve-outs*. Regulators issue general licences to permit certain flows—disaster aid, medical payments—without fear of secondary sanctions. That mitigates blunt harm, but at a cost. Compliance teams must model intent, proof, and record-keeping; NGOs must route around blacklists without triggering false positives. The friction is measurable: more hours per transaction, more documentation per dollar, and a higher rate of bank de-risking. In 2021–2023, aid groups documented repeated account closures in sanctioned jurisdictions despite licences, because intermediaries priced the risk of error above the benefit of service. Carve-outs reduce pain. They also institutionalise hesitancy.

The second counter-example is technical: *privacy layers*. Tools from basic mixers to sophisticated zero-knowledge systems can obfuscate flows. They protect dissidents and whistle-blowers; they also shelter crime. When OFAC sanctioned Tornado Cash, the sanction did not turn code into a person. It nevertheless chilled a whole category of privacy use because interfaces, relays, and middleware feared liability. Mitigations—selective disclosure proofs, tiered privacy for small payments—reintroduced the language of proportion. Yet each mitigation increased complexity and cost. Users paid higher fees; developers maintained dual paths; auditors learned new cryptography. Privacy was not free; it printed a receipt.

To evaluate enforcement or evasion coherently, pair abstractions with *metrics*. Trust becomes the *false positive rate* of compliance screens and the *time to clear* for legitimate users. Efficiency becomes the *median confirmation time* across censored and non-censored paths and the *variance* during stress. Risk becomes the *ex-ante loss* if a provider freezes a percentage of flows and the *ex-post recovery rate* after appeal. Publish these numbers and the debate leaves ideology. It enters accountability.

CBDCs alter the field. A retail CBDC can hard-code constraints—transaction ceilings, merchant categories, expiry dates—turning policy into programmable state. That grants tools to target aid precisely, throttle money velocity, or block sanctioned entities at the point of payment. It also centralises the chokepoint. Ask: who writes the conditions, who audits the logs, and what opt-out exists? The answers split along governance lines. A two-tier architecture with privacy by default for small transactions and layered disclosure for larger ones distributes power and reduces data hoarding. A single-tier system with full traceability concentrates both risk and discretion. Each path prices freedom differently.

Stablecoins—especially dollar-backed ones—expand enforcement range by fusing legal authority with programmable controls. When an issuer blacklists an address, the token obeys everywhere it circulates. The speed is impressive. So is the overhang. Liquidity providers face tail risk: a counterparty could be frozen mid-cycle. DeFi protocols inherit transformer risk: wrapped assets can turn to stone inside pools when issuers act. A rational response is *address hygiene*: proactive screening, route choice, and caps on exposure to tokens with unilateral freeze functions. But hygiene has limits. The more aggressively issuers police flows, the greater the incentive for shadow liquidity that avoids banks and regulated on-ramps altogether. Enforcement that wins the battle can lose the network.

Bridges complicate the calculus. A sanctioned address can rinse a claim through a permissive chain, then return via a trusted bridge as a "clean" asset—unless the bridge enforces origin checks. Many do not, or cannot, at scale. Where they do, throughput slows and costs rise. Where they don't, risk propagates. The obvious fix—light-client verification with proof-carrying messages—raises engineering cost and narrows compatibility. The less obvious fix—*rate limits* and *circuit breakers* when suspicious flows spike—moves us back to policy at the edge. Either way, the *chokepoint*—bridge operators and custodians—returns as the decisive actor.

The cat learns; the mouse adapts. Exchanges now share intelligence through industry consortia; wallets warn users when they interact with high-risk addresses; providers internalise the price of sanctions risk by adjusting fees. The visible behaviour is *premium pricing* for compliance. Users who want guarantees pay more in spread and slippage; those who want speed accept higher audit risk. This segmentation mirrors credit markets: safer paper trades cheaper. The implication is less romance, more triage. A multipolar monetary internet devolves into tiers of cleanliness and convenience.

Two further episodes sharpen the point. In April 2018, BNP Paribas' $8.9 billion settlement for sanctions violations formalised a lesson for global banks: U.S. jurisdiction follows the dollar. That incentivised *de-risking* across vast swathes of Africa and parts of the Caribbean, where smaller banks lost correspondent lines not for violations but for perceived fragility in compliance. Meanwhile, in 2023–2024, the mBridge project—a BIS-convened trial linking Hong Kong, Thailand, the UAE and others—demonstrated prototype cross-border CBDC settlement. The show here is not a finished product but a direction: enforcement and evasion will move into *rails*, not only *rules*. As rails diversify, so do pressure points.

The motif of the *chokepoint* returns in an unexpected place: cloud. Many nodes, relays, and analytics stacks run on a handful of cloud providers. Subpoenas, account closures, or quiet policy nudges can degrade network capacity without touching consensus. The behaviour is mundane—rate limits, API changes, region restrictions. The implication is strategic: operational decentralisation—multi-cloud, self-hosted critical components, geographic spread—is a sanctions resilience measure, not mere DevOps fussiness. Freedom has uptime metrics.

What would *credible proportion* look like? Three visible behaviours. First, *bounded data*: collect only what is needed for the stated purpose, store it locally when feasible, and delete on schedule. Second, *tiered controls*: small payments presumptively private with immediate settlement; larger ones subject to explicit proofs or reviews. Third, *auditable restraint*: publish statistics on blocks filtered, addresses frozen, appeals granted, and time to resolution. These are not soft virtues. They operationalise the claim that enforcement targets *bad acts* rather than *broad categories*. Without them, the line between policy and punishment blurs.

None of this dissolves the paradox at the core of sanctions. To be effective, sanctions must raise the cost of prohibited behaviour, including by harming networks that service it. To be legitimate, sanctions must minimise collateral damage to ordinary life. Cat wants the corridor narrow; mouse needs it wide enough for medicine, remittances, and dissent. The space in between is hard law and harder engineering.

The limits of evasion must be faced plainly. Routing through privacy tech can shield activists, but it also paints targets when interfaces flag "risky behaviour." Self-custody can resist arbitrary freezes, but it shifts the burden of security to individuals who may lack the means. Peer-to-peer markets can reduce exposure to chokepoints, but they expose participants to scams and violent crime. Each counter-move prints a receipt. The question is whether the price matches the value.

So the forward test becomes institutional, not ideological. If a ministry can freeze assets, can it also be compelled—by statute and interface—to log, notify, and allow appeal within fixed timeframes? If a stablecoin issuer can blacklist, can it also publish a verifiable ledger of freezes, unfreezes, and legal bases? If a relay filters, can proposers bypass it quickly with acceptable revenue loss? If an NGO operates under general licences, can its bank measure and report the false positive rate and show improvement? These are design choices masquerading as policy. They are also policy choices masquerading as design.

The *chokepoint* motif ends with a practical image. Imagine every enforcement lever as a valve with a pressure gauge. Enforcement can close a valve, but must watch the gauge. If pressure builds—fees spike, inclusion times drift, false positives climb—you either open the valve a turn or build a bypass. If the gauge lies, the pipe bursts somewhere else. The cat can win a move. It cannot end the game. The only stable settlement is proportionate, measured, and instrumented—because on a monetary internet, every squeeze has a signature, and every signature finds a route.

Resilience Through Redundancy

On 20 September 2017 in San Juan, two days after Hurricane Maria made landfall, power vanished across Puerto Rico. ATMs went dark. Card terminals blinked and died. Supermarkets that could open took cash only; fuel stations rationed by hand-written receipt. For weeks, money functioned where electrons did not. The island relearned an old lesson: robustness is a function of spares. Keep a second path.

On 8 November 2016 in New Delhi, India's government announced that ₹500 and ₹1,000 notes would cease to be legal tender. Overnight, 86 per cent of the cash in circulation became problematic. Queues formed; wages went unpaid; small firms bartered to survive. Digital wallets surged, then faltered when telecom coverage or KYC throttled access. The policy aim was legitimate. The single-point dependency on cash was not. Again, the missing element was a second path: another medium, another rail, another custody.

Second path is the quiet motif of this subchapter. Redundancy—across monies, custodians, and modes of access—turns fragility into inconvenience. It is not glamorous. It is deeply civic. It keeps households, firms, and clinics functional irrespective of policy or outage. The craft is to define redundancy not as redundancy of logos, but of *assumptions*.

Show → Name → Explain → Implication. Start with layered monies. A resilient community holds *more than one* spendable asset across *more than one* trust model: local currency cash for outage resilience; bank deposits for payroll and large transfers; a stablecoin for cross-border settlement; a censorship-resistant asset for capital flight and high-friction emergencies. Name the behaviour: families in Lagos using naira for groceries, USDT for rent protection, and small Bitcoin balances for contingency. Explain the mechanism: each layer fails differently—cash with theft and fire; banks with freezes and holidays; stablecoins with issuer or bank risk; censorship-resistant assets with volatility and learning cost. Implication: diversification across monetary *failure modes* is insurance against policy surprises and physical shocks.

A second show: custody diversity. In June 2022, crypto exchanges tightened withdrawal policies as markets whipsawed and lenders paused redemptions. Users with keys in cold storage had options; those relying on custodial accounts did not. Name the instruments: multisignature wallets splitting authorisation across devices or people; social recovery with guardians; custody with multiple regulated providers in distinct jurisdictions; and, for ordinary citizens, simple hardware devices with printed backups stored off-site. Explain the point: custody is not a binary of "self" or "other" but a spectrum of *who can say no* to your transaction. Implication: the more routes that must align to block you, the less any single failure can do.

Third show: offline modes. In Nigeria, the eNaira launched in October 2021 added a USSD interface to allow transactions without smartphones. In South Africa and neighbouring countries, the Machankura project (2022) let users send small Bitcoin payments over basic GSM using USSD codes. In 2018, Blockstream Satellite expanded its broadcast of Bitcoin blocks to multiple continents, enabling reception without the public internet; earlier, goTenna and Samourai's TxTenna experiment demonstrated mesh relays for transaction broadcast. Name the behaviour: transact when the grid is unstable. Explain the affordance: *local* liveness—short-range or unilateral receipt—when broader networks are down. Implication: monetary continuity need not be digital perfection; it needs *enough* connectivity to keep essentials moving.

Pair abstractions with measurements. *Trust* becomes the *reversal rate* under stress and the *share of transactions* that settle via an alternative path when the main rail stalls. *Efficiency* becomes *median time to pay* across modalities—card, cash, stablecoin—when networks degrade. *Risk* becomes *percentage of household savings* accessible without internet for a week, and *days of cash on hand* in supply chains. Institutions that measure these can govern for continuity, not just for compliance.

Redundancy is not a slogan; it is design. Consider *layered monies* in practice. In the eurozone, a digital euro may eventually include offline functionality for small transactions. If designed with tiered privacy and caps, it could act as state-level redundancy to private networks, preserving cash-like resilience while enabling policy tools. In parallel, banks could commit to *cash stewardship targets*—days of currency available per branch—and publish outage drills. Firms could maintain a small float of stablecoins with published redemption arrangements and counterparty mappings. The point is not ideology. It is posture: assume electricity dies, routers fail, and policy shifts.

A credible counter-example tests the thesis. Redundancy can create *attack surface*. More wallets, more backups, and more rails mean more ways to make mistakes or be robbed. Offline modes may ease fraud; paper backups can be stolen; multisig guardians can collude. Reconcile this by scope and constraint. Set *caps* for offline and low-assurance paths; use *time locks* and *spending limits* on hot wallets; restrict guardianship to trusted circles with periodic checks; and audit flows with *receipts* that list who approved what, when. Redundancy that grows without discipline becomes entropy. Redundancy that is bounded becomes resilience.

Return to custody diversity with a second named, checkable example. During the Canadian trucker protests in February 2022, some bank accounts were temporarily frozen under emergency powers; several centralised crowdfunding platforms also restricted payouts. Regardless of one's view on the politics, the operational lesson was clear: custody concentration is a policy fuse. Merchants who used multiple processors, or who kept a portion of liquidity in alternative rails, maintained more optionality. This is not an argument against lawful enforcement. It is an argument for *continuity by design*, especially for NGOs and small businesses that cannot afford multi-week gaps.

Resilience has a supply-chain analogue. Pharmacies, grocers, and fuel distributors can model *clearance under outage*: how many goods can be sold for cash or via offline token vouchers before reconciliation. A city's transport authority can commit to an *offline fare* mode that runs for seventy-two hours without central servers. Measurement makes the ethic concrete: drills every quarter, published times to clear, visible caps. If the numbers are embarrassing, the design needs amendment.

Layered monies also limit *policy whiplash*. When exchange controls, capital limits, or demonetisation arrive, societies with multiple working monies adapt faster. Argentina's freelancers who invoice in stablecoins and settle expenses locally are practising shock absorption. Kenyan merchants who accept both M-Pesa and cash routinely switch rails during network hiccups. The behaviour is not exotic. It is simply *having a second path*.

We should resist the false comfort that redundancy is a niche requirement for fragile states. High-income systems depend on concentrated providers—clouds, card schemes, core banking platforms. Their reliability is extraordinary; their correlation is higher than it appears. A concentrated cloud outage in a single region can degrade a surprising share of issuers and acquirers. A routing update in a major ISP can strand an entire class of terminals. The metric here is *correlated downtime*. If your top three vendors share the same upstream dependencies, you don't have three vendors. You have one vendor thrice.

Offline modes deserve a harder look. They are often treated as marketing, not muscle. An *offline CBDC* must be cash-like at small values: local settlement with tamper-evident devices, deferred synchronisation, and theft-bounded caps. A *card fall-back* must allow floor limits with rapid risk-based tuning and clear liability. A *stablecoin wallet* that claims offline should print or display a *pre-authorised token*, not merely queue an intent. Each modality needs a *fraud budget*: the maximum tolerable loss during outages, priced into operations rather than wished away. The civic equation is explicit: small, fast, private payments at the edge; audited reconciliation at the core.

Diverse custody extends beyond individuals. Institutions can avoid capture by splitting roles. A charity operating in a sanctioned region can keep local funds in cash and mobile money, store contingency value in a multi-sig with international guardians, and maintain a small bank float in a neutral jurisdiction. Each pool fails under different pressures. Each pool has a different *denial path*. Publish these models as part of organisational governance and donors can judge competence rather than ideology.

The motif of the *second path* applies to identity as well. Account recovery is a monetary function. If the only path to regain access is a single platform's helpdesk, your money depends on a queue. Social recovery with three guardians in two countries is a second path. Legal recourse via a trustee is another. A government-issued offline credential stored on a chip card, used only for small private payments, is another. Each choice should be legible in an interface—*who can say no*—so that users understand the politics of their recovery flows.

There is an art to avoiding *redundancy theatre*. Owning three wallets that all rely on the same cloud and the same relay is not diversity. Holding cash in one drawer and the same cash in another is not layering. A credible scheme maps *assumptions*: power, connectivity, jurisdiction, and institutional discretion. Then it picks *orthogonal* counterparts—different utilities, different rails, different legal regimes. The test is operational: drill for loss of power, drill for loss of cloud, drill for loss of goodwill. Time the exits. Count the taps. Measure the clearance.

We should also be candid about costs. Redundancy consumes attention. It asks for training. It introduces friction. Citizens already overloaded by precarious work and complex bureaucracy cannot be expected to become their own treasurers. The reconciliation is *defaults with disclosures*. Make safe redundancy the default—small offline balances enabled, exportable recovery phrases presented and practised, multi-provider routing automatic at the edge—while preserving a clear path to "simple mode" for those who need it. Interfaces can teach, gently. Receipts can summarise, plainly. Training is policy.

History supports the claim that redundancy is civic infrastructure. During cash shortages after demonetisation in India (November 2016), small merchants who could toggle between wallets, bank transfers, and cash survived better. After Hurricane Maria (September 2017), communities with diesel reserves for generators and paper ledgers for rationing cleared essentials faster. In both cases, formal policy mattered. Informal preparedness decided outcomes.

The second path returns as closing image. Imagine a city as a mesh, not a line. Grocers can sell for cash or tokens; buses accept offline payments for three days; clinics can pay staff from a local float; remittances arrive on at least two rails; citizens know, roughly, how to export a key. None of this removes the need for strong policy. It removes the need for *perfect* policy. It buys time.

The forward test is merciless and simple. If power fails for a week, which bills still get paid? If a bank holiday is declared, which payrolls still run? If a stablecoin issuer pauses redemptions, which families still remit across borders? If one cloud region degrades, which terminals still accept? Design for credible answers now, and redundancy will feel like over-engineering—until the hour it feels like mercy. The second path is not a luxury. It is the constitution of continuity.

Freedom, Finally, as a Practice

On 15 October 2020 in Lagos, bank accounts linked to the Feminist Coalition were frozen during the #EndSARS protests. Within days the group published new donation routes, including a Bitcoin address and, later, a pay-to-URL payment page. The outcome was plain: inflows resumed; food, legal aid, and medical supplies reached streets where ATMs were failing and point-of-sale terminals flickered. A slogan about freedom had met an institution—the banking system—and adjusted. Habits decide who copes well.

The Lagos episode is not an outlier. In March 2013, depositors in Nicosia learnt that their savings in Cyprus Popular Bank would be bailed in under an emergency deal; withdrawals were capped, transfers controlled, and expectations rewritten. In February 2022, Ottawa's emergency powers froze some accounts linked to a protest movement; several platforms halted disbursements. These are different contexts with different rights and wrongs. They share a lesson: freedom that survives contact is organised. It knows institutions by name, and it drills.

The quiet motif of this subchapter is *rehearsal*. Not theatre. Muscle memory. Freedom becomes durable when we embed it in routines that withstand outages, orders, and errors. Institutional literacy articulates the stage—how banks reconcile, how payment processors prioritise, how wallets and validators can be leaned on. Disciplined design writes the script—defaults that bias to exit, custody that resists capture, privacy that is earned not assumed. Rehearsal makes the two meet.

Show → Name → Explain → Implication. Start with a visible behaviour: using more than one ledger willingly. Name the pattern: layered balances across cash, bank deposits, stablecoins, and a censorship-resistant reserve. Explain the mechanism: each layer fails differently. Cash fails with theft and fire; bank accounts fail with policy and outages; stablecoins fail with issuer freezes or banking stress; censorship-resistant assets fail with volatility and key loss. The implication is practical. Institutional literacy is not "knowing crypto". It is understanding failure modes, and structuring habits so no single institution can define your horizon.

The second behaviour is *time-bounded dependency*. A self-employed designer in Buenos Aires that invoices in DAI or USDC, converts weekly to pesos to pay suppliers, and holds a small BTC reserve is not making a statement. She is measuring exposure. She aims for a *time-to-survive* if any rail stalls: seven days if the exchange halts, three if the ISP drops, one if a merchant network chokes. Freedom is a budget in days and hops. It is the calendar, not the placard.

The third behaviour is *receipts*. Not the paper kind, but systematic proofs. A charity operating in Yangon under licence conditions documents the false-positive rate of its bank's sanctions screening—how many legitimate payments were flagged, how long they took to clear—and publishes a monthly summary to donors. An NGO in

Kharkiv that pays stipends over mesh-friendly wallets audits what settled during a week of power cuts, how many retries were needed, and what share of its reserves could move without cloud providers. The numbers are not decoration. They are how literacy becomes governance. If you cannot measure your chokepoints, someone else will.

Rehearsal matters at protocol level too. In October 2020, the People's Bank of China's e-CNY pilots in Shenzhen demonstrated *programmable distribution* at scale. The state rehearsed targeted disbursement; the public rehearsed new forms of traceability. In August 2021, Ethereum's EIP-1559 began burning base fees, making supply responsive to network use. Each changed daily habits: which fees users bid, which wallets showed, which dashboards communities used to judge health. The institutional literacy here is unromantic. Understand what a protocol guarantees, what it measures, and who can flip which switch. Then design your use so the switches do not define you.

A credible counter-example tempers zeal. El Salvador's September 2021 law making Bitcoin legal tender promised sovereign exit from dollar dependency. Adoption remained low; many citizens withdrew the initial Chivo wallet bonus and returned to cash or dollars. The reasons were human: user trust, merchant UX, intermittent connectivity, and fear of volatility. Reconcile the lesson honestly. Freedom that is decreed from above can seed capacity, but without *practised* habits—stable pricing, reliable support, obvious recourse—the muscle withers. Institutional literacy must be household literacy, not ministerial ambition.

Discipline sounds austere. It is, in fact, humane. Consider *key management.* A family in Nairobi storing a modest emergency reserve on a hardware wallet with social recovery guardians—two relatives abroad and one local lawyer—has turned a fragile secret into a shared, bounded trust. The design choice is precise: a three-of-five threshold, time delays on resets, and a printed recovery walkthrough rehearsed at the kitchen table twice a year. The visible metrics are simple: time to recovery under loss; number of people who can stall a malicious reset; days the reserve can fund essentials. This is not ideology. It is domestic policy.

Discipline also reassigns power through interface. In 2023, several consumer wallets added warnings when users interacted with addresses labelled high risk by analytics providers. Good. But literacy demands counterweights: a path to challenge, a clear explanation of the label's basis, and a timer that shows expected resolution if the system is wrong. If a payment is blocked, the app should print a *justification receipt* stating whether the block was policy, provider preference, or user setting. Freedom is not only the ability to send. It is the ability to know why something does not send. The metric to track is the *appeal cycle time*—from block to explanation to remedy.

Practice requires *plural custody*. In 2022, when several crypto lenders suspended withdrawals, users who held assets at a single custodian learnt that "not your keys" was less a motto than a recovery plan they had not rehearsed. A disciplined scheme splits liquidity: an exchange account for convenience, a regulated custodian for large balances with insurance and clear jurisdiction, and a self-custody wallet for reserves with time locks. No single relationship should be able to freeze your entire life. Again, receipts. Document who can deny; document how to exit; drill the process quarterly. If it takes twelve steps and a ticket to withdraw, you haven't rehearsed. You have hoped.

Institutions can practise too. A mid-sized university in Accra that receives grants in foreign currency sets up a treasury playbook: stablecoin accounts with two independent issuers, a local bank with FX capacity, and a multi-sig reserve with guardians in different countries. It drills for a bank holiday by paying a week's payroll over alternative rails; it measures slippage, failure rate, and staff complaints. The goal is not to embarrass providers. It is to identify which valves stick. Freedom at scale is boring. It is also public.

Rehearsal should include *privacy literacy*. After OFAC's Tornado Cash designation (August 2022), many tools defaulted to geofencing and address filtering. The lived effect was that lawful, privacy-seeking users got caught in dragnet logic. A disciplined design for privacy does not promise invisibility. It promises *proportion*: small payments private by default with audit on consent; higher-risk flows gated by selective disclosure proofs; explicit warnings when a path invites scrutiny. The metrics to watch are the *privacy failure rate*—how often legitimate small payments leak identifying data—and the *proof acceptance rate*—how often verifiers accept well-formed disclosures without manual escalation. Freedom loses legitimacy when it hides abuse. It loses reality when it hides from measurement.

The rehearsal motif returns in the dullest, most decisive place: *upgrades*. When a protocol or wallet changes assumptions, does it stage a constitutional moment or a stealth patch? Ethereum's Merge in September 2022 had years of public testing, viewable roadmaps, and exit options for dissenters. That is institutional literacy in action: change acknowledged as governance. By contrast, when a centralised bridge quietly adjusts withdrawal rules after an incident, users learn about sovereignty the hard way. Discipline demands that critical changes print receipts: what changed, who approved, how to exit, and what the rollback plan is. The habit to cultivate is *reading the changelog* before reading the marketing page.

We should resist the comforting myth that practice is for the marginal. Wealthy households, established firms, and "stable" jurisdictions often rely on invisible monopolies: a single card network, a single cloud region, a single identity provider. When a routing update or regional outage occurs, sophisticated people become as helpless as anyone else. Freedom as habit is a class leveller. It asks the same questions of everyone: how many exits, how fast, with what receipts?

Naming the abstraction "freedom" invites misuse. So name the decisions instead. How much of your liquidity settles under local law, and how much under foreign? Which providers can deny you service without appeal? What percentage of your payables can you execute if you lose power for seventy-two hours? How long does it take to export your keys, your contacts, your invoices? These are policies for households as much as for states. The measure is not bravery. It is clearance under stress.

A final example sharpens the stakes. In 2023, the BIS's "mBridge" trials linked several monetary authorities to test cross-border CBDC settlement. The architecture, if adopted, will encode policy at the rail. Fine. But an exporter in Dubai or Bangkok, depending solely on that rail, will be exposed to a single cluster's outages and policies. A disciplined exporter rehearses a second path: stablecoin settlement with documented redemption rights, a correspondent route with pre-cleared limits, and a self-custody reserve priced for volatility. The discipline is costed. The benefit is sleep.

Freedom as a practice will disappoint those who want romance. It looks like quarterly drills, dull receipts, and interfaces that insist you read. It sounds like family meetings and runbooks. It feels like carrying a second card and a small float. It is measured in *time-to-function* when policy or power wobbles. The payoff is that slogans stop being necessary. The habits hold.

The forward test is blunt. If your preferred rail halts tonight, what moves by morning, at what price, with which receipts? If a change in law reclassifies your asset, what exits without a phone call? If your wallet blocks a payment, how long to a reason? If you cannot answer in minutes rather than myths, you have a plan in theory, not a practice in hand. Rehearse until the answers become muscle.

About the Author

Nicolette Sharma writes about money as a human institution before it is a spreadsheet. Her work follows a simple conviction: how we design and govern our currencies shapes who is visible, who is vulnerable, and who is free. Raised among multiple languages and exchange rates, she learned early that value is always negotiated—sometimes by law, sometimes by custom, and increasingly by code. Drawing on economic history, political thought, and the craft of clear explanation, she guides readers through contested terrain without evangelism or cynicism. Her aim is to build public judgement: practical ways to tell resilience from hype when money moves from mint to machine.

www.ingramcontent.com/pod-product-compliance
Lightning Source LLC
Chambersburg PA
CBHW031345230926
51848CB00002B/395
9789374596340